Cambridge First Certificate
Examination Practice 4

Teacher's Book

Cambridge
First Certificate

Examination
Practice 4

Teacher's Book

University of Cambridge
Local Examinations Syndicate

CAMBRIDGE
UNIVERSITY PRESS

Published by the Press Syndicate of the University of Cambridge
The Pitt Building, Trumpington Street, Cambridge CB2 1RP
40 West 20th Street, New York, NY 10011–4211, USA
10 Stamford Road, Oakleigh, Victoria 3166, Australia

© Cambridge University Press 1991

First published 1991
Reprinted 1992

Printed in Great Britain at the University Press, Cambridge

ISBN 0 521 407354 Teacher's Book
ISBN 0 521 408342 Student's Book
ISBN 0 521 407338 Set of 2 cassettes

Contents

Introduction

The tests in *Cambridge First Certificate Examination Practice 4* are designed to familiarise students with the style and format of the First Certificate in English (FCE) examination papers and to provide them with practice in examination techniques. The tests can be used in class for pre-examination practice and discussion, as 'mock examinations', or by students working alone using the Teacher's Book as a key. The tests are reproduced exactly as they appear in the examination.

A suggested mark scheme for each of the tests is provided in the Teacher's Book, but it must be emphasised that no fully authoritative assessment of students can be based on this. In the FCE examination itself a series of complex statistical procedures is carried out to correlate a candidate's performance in all five papers, and such procedures cannot be accurately reproduced by the teacher working alone.

The current FCE examination syllabus was introduced in 1975 and modified in 1984. Broadly speaking, there are four different ideas underlying the syllabus:

a) the now universal acceptance of communicative approaches in the EFL classroom, which is reflected in and, indeed, encouraged by the FCE examination;
b) the increased prominence of listening and speaking skills in classrooms, reflected in the one-third weighting in the examination;
c) the view that reading and listening texts should be taken from authentic sources within a candidate's range of experience, and not be specifically written, abridged or over-literary;
d) the need to avoid culture bias in the examination, confirming the status of English as an international language.

The ways in which these ideas are embodied in the examination itself are outlined on pages 2 to 13 and can be seen in the practice tests in the Student's Book.

The Teacher's Book contains:
– a suggested mark scheme and answer key for each paper;
– complete transcripts of the recorded Listening Comprehension tests;
– instructions on the handling of the Interview.

The two accompanying cassettes contain the recordings for the Listening Comprehension tests: the tests cannot be used without the appropriate cassette.

The First Certificate Examination

The chart below gives an outline of how each paper of the FCE examination is assessed. In the examination the final assessment of any candidate is reached only on the basis of total performance in all five papers and after the marks have been carefully correlated and adjusted to establish correct weightings and grading levels. Adjustments are also made to offset the effect of random guessing in multiple-choice and true/false questions. Such procedures are clearly impracticable for the teacher working alone. However, the information in the chart below and throughout the Teacher's Book can be used as a guide to an approximate assessment of a candidate's likely level of performance.

The complete examination carries a total of 180 marks.

Name of paper	Time	Total marks	Assessment
Paper 1 Reading Comprehension	1 hour	40	A mark contributing to a pass grading in the whole examination is normally about 60% of the possible score for this paper.
Paper 2 Composition	1½ hours	40	An impression mark is given, following a grading scale for each composition. On average, pass candidates score about 40% of the total and very good candidates 75–90%.
Paper 3 Use of English	2 hours	40	This paper is marked according to a detailed scale and on an impression mark for the final question. On average, pass candidates score 50–60% of the paper total.
Paper 4 Listening Comprehension	30 to 40 minutes	20	This paper is marked according to a detailed mark scheme with varied weightings for items. On average, pass candidates score about 60% of the paper total.
Paper 5 Interview	15 to 20 minutes	40	An impression mark is given on each of six grading scales. On average, pass candidates score about 60% of the paper total.

Paper 1: Reading Comprehension (1 hour)

Paper 1 is in multiple-choice form, with four-choice items as follows: Section A with 25 questions, each consisting of a sentence with a blank to be filled, and Section B with 15 questions on three or more reading passages.

Section A tests candidates' knowledge of English vocabulary (including synonyms, antonyms, collocations and phrasal verbs) as well as their knowledge of grammatical rules and constraints.

Section B tests candidates' general understanding of the gist of passages as well as their understanding of specific information given. The passages vary in length, character and density and are drawn from a variety of authentic sources, including fiction, non-fiction, newspapers, magazines, brochures, leaflets and advertisements. The third passage may include information presented in a diagram, map or chart.

Candidates record their answers to Paper 1 on a separate answer sheet, **not** on the question paper. A sample answer sheet for Paper 1 can be found at the back of the Student's Book.

Marking

Section A carries a total possible mark of 25; the 15 questions in Section B count **double**, giving a final raw total (scaled to 40) of 55. An incorrect answer gains no mark, but no marks are specifically deducted for wrong answers. The final 'raw' total of 55 is scaled down to a maximum of 40.

Exam preparation

It is important not to practise this type of test to excess, but merely to accustom students to its requirements and tempo. Multiple-choice questions have more value as a testing device than as a teaching method, and excessive practice in doing this type of test is unlikely to improve students' ability to read English more efficiently. Time should be devoted in class, therefore, to improving students' reading skills and not just their ability to answer reading comprehension questions.

Students should be given experience of reading authentic texts of the kind shown in Cambridge First Certificate Examination Practice 4 and given help in learning how to understand them. Such help may include teaching students how to understand the gist of a passage and how to extract the main points of information from it without necessarily understanding every single word they read.

Paper 2: Composition (1½ hours)

From a choice of five topics, two compositions – each of between 120 and 180 words – are to be written in the 1½ hours allotted. The choice of topics includes a letter, a description, a narrative, a straightforward discursive composition, or quasi-spoken language in the form of a speech or monologue. There is an additional choice of topic based on optional reading, as specified in the examination Regulations for each year.

The advantage for candidates of choosing to read one of the books selected for the exam is that it may offer them an enjoyable and worthwhile reading experience, increasing language awareness, as well as a wider range of topics to choose from in Paper 2. Candidates also have the chance to discuss their reading of one of the texts in the Interview, if they wish (see page 82).

Marking

An impression mark out of 20 is given for each composition, using the scale shown below. This mark is based on an overall impression of the language used, including the range and appropriateness of vocabulary, sentence and paragraph structure and correctness of grammar, spelling and punctuation. Individual mistakes are not penalised but count in the overall impression. It is the language used, not the content, which is the main concern, and marks are not deducted for unorthodox opinions or illogical arguments. However, the inclusion of irrelevant material which seems to have been learnt by heart does lose marks. Over-short compositions will lose marks, as may over-long ones because they often contain more mistakes or are badly structured. The chart below shows the scale used to assess each composition.

	Language	Task
18–20	Natural English with minimal errors.	Full realisation of task.
16–17	More than a collection of simple sentences, with good vocabulary and structures. Some occasional lapses.	
11–15	Sufficient naturalness of English and not many errors.	Simple but accurate realisation of the task.
8–10	Communication established despite some errors.	Task reasonably attempted.
5–7	Lack of control/frequent basic errors.	Task only partly realised (by neglect of the rubric).
1–4	Incoherence.	Gross irrelevance, and/or too short for language assessment.

The following sample compositions taken from the Syndicate's reports illustrate the quality of language which typifies candidates in the six categories indicated above.

18 MARKS

What do you think have been the main changes in people's lives since your grandparents were young?

My grandparents were born in the twenties of this century. During these last sixty years, a lot of changes have occurred in people's lives, due to the scientific and technological progress.

The everyday life has become easier: the means of transport have been improved and travel has become quicker and safer; there has been more comfort in the houses, and in general, the human beings' conditions have lost much of their toughness. Medicine has made a great step forward and all sorts of inventions – which my grandparents couldn't even dream of have become a reality.

On the other hand, the means of destruction have been improved, too: bombs and weapons are now much more efficient. Some illnesses are still incurable, and others, which were completely unknown sixty years ago, have appeared. There is less manual work now – but people have become more and more nervous. Obviously, the progress has got its price.

With respect to these changes, and as far as the most important aim of the humanity seems to be the progress, a question should be asked: are people now happier than before?

Examiner's comments:
This composition shows an ability to control structure and use appropriate lexis. There is evidence of a planned approach to the topic.

4

The following two pairs of compositions show how candidates of different abilities treated the same topic.

The information a travel agent gave you about your recent holiday was wrong. Write a letter to him describing the problems you had.

16 MARKS

27, rue Pierre Leroux
75007 Paris

13 June, 1988

Dear Sir,

    I have just arrived from Spain where I spent the last month on holiday and I am writing to you to complain about the information you gave me concerning my holiday.

    You told me you had booked a room for me in "the best hotel of Barcelona," – I even remember your own words! Arriving there, I was very disappointed to see that the hotel was a small dark one situated in a dirty usafe quarter. And, to my horror, I was told that no room had been booked for me. They even didn't know who you are!

    In addition, the woman whose address you gave me and who was supposed to be my interpreter had left her place ten months ago!

    I wouldn't tell you how difficult it was to find a hotel and how silly I felt being alone and unable to make myself understood!

    There is no need either to tell you that I had an awful holiday and you are entirely responsible of that. I will soon write to the manager and ask him to take the right measures against you.

Yours sincerely,

Examiner's comments:
Despite minor grammatical and lexical lapses the candidate has tackled the task very well and used appropriate style and vocabulary. A sound piece of work.

8 MARKS

29 Mill Field
Folkestone
Kent CT20 1EU

14 June, 1988

London Travel
10 London Road
London W1

Dear Sir,

    I am writing to complain about the information that you gave me about my holiday. When I booked it, you told me that the deperture of flight was 9.00pm, but the information I received today show me that it is 9.00am.

    If the deperture time had been the morning, I wouldn't have decided to go, because I live in Folkestone now and it takes me more than two hours to get to Gatwick by train. (I always use train, because it is cheaper than taxi.) Also when people use aeroplane, they must check in by one and a half hours before the deperture. If the deperture time is 9.00am, I must get up at 5.00am. As you know I am 60 years old, and as I get tired easily, it is very hard for me to get up in the early morning. So whenever I go on holiday, I decide my holiday according to the departure time of flight. Though I used to stay a hotel and spend one night before so as not to be tired, I think it is that I lose my money.

    Could you change the flight time, or if not so, could you possibly refund my money for my holiday?

    I look forward to hearing from you.
      Yours faithfully,

Examiner's comments:
A confused account because of inability to use tenses correctly. The holiday is not over so the task has not been completed satisfactorily. (−2 marks for this: 10−2=8)

Imagine you have been called up to do military service. How will you spend your last day of freedom as a civilian?

15 MARKS

In most countries, military service is an obligation (for men). You have to spend about one year of your life inside the walls of a military base. Most of the men are "allergic" to this idea and can't get used to the idea of beeing "cut" from the world, family and friends, and live in a place where you can't think, you can only obbey.

As far as I'm concerned, I'll spend my last day of freedom with all my mates and my family. I think that giving a party is the best way to say goodbye in a pleasant atmosphere of fun and happiness No tears, no regrets, only laughs, jokes, music, and pints of beer until the last minute of freedom. Everybody has to enjoy the party. In a way It'll be like the last day of freedom before getting married when you say goodbye to your childhood. After the military service, you won't be a boy anymore but a man.

Examiner's comments:
There are some good ideas here which are reasonably well ordered. There are, however, some basic structural errors.

10 MARKS

Dear Diary,

I've just been called to do my military service and I only have one day left before I leave.
I'll get up early tomorrow so that I can do everything I planned before leaving.
Before breakfast I'll go for a jogg in the park with my brother to fix the beautiful lake and the flowers in my memory Then I'll have breakfast with all the family as usual. Mummy will boil me an egg, cook some bacon and make a whole tea pot. I want to remember the smells and the atmosphere of that moment of the day.
Then I'll go to visit my grandmother to say goodbye and tell her I'd miss her while I'm gone.
Then I'll phone John, my best friend, and ask him to go to the museum and have lunch with me. I may phone Richard as well.
After that I'll call Sally to invite her to the cinema and will both come back home to have supper with all my family. I'll probably go to bed early because my train is leaving at 9 a.m
Goodbye!

Examiner's comments:
A clear simple account with a few errors. A definite pass but not extended enough to get it into a higher category.

11 MARKS

You are asked to give a talk to a group of school children on the importance of road safety. What advice do you give them?

Listen to me please! will you? You have never seen me before but pay attention, because what I am going to tell you is very important. What I want to explain to you is how staying safe in the street. In fact it is not complicate you have just to respect some easy rules. It is like a game. All of you have remarked that our streets are very busy with many lorries, cars and motorbikes. That is just the reason for which you have to be careful. At any time, a car can knock you down if you are not careful neither the driver is.

First, cross every street at zebra crossing. Before crossing look right and left, if there is no traffic light. If you are afraid of being knocked down ask an adult for help. If there is a traffic light wait until the light turns green for pedestrians. Never cross roundabout, highway and very busy streets without an adult, anyway don't do it! It is the most dangerous thing to do.

Second, walk always on the pavement. If you are with your mother hold her hand and keep it! On the pavement if you are not running, playing football or playing with a ball, there is no risks of being knocked down by any vehicule. Anyway we never know what could happen, consequently, in the street, be careful! That is the best advice I can give. Be always aware of the danger, and never forget that vehicules can kill. Thank you for listening to me, next time we will speak about how staying safe at home.

Examiner's comments:
A reasonable attempt to complete the task using the appropriate register. This is marred by frequent errors which make for confusing reading at times.

6 MARKS

Describe a day at work or at school when everything went wrong. Explain what happened to you and how the day ended.

It was five years ago in a little town, in south of France, just before an exam. It was a sunny day and very warm too.
As we were seating in our classroom, we had sawn suddenly our headmaster rushed into the class and ordered us not to panic.
It was right away very agitated.
Then, he asked us to take all our things and go very quickly in the middle of the school yard.
We were wondering what was happening while we were running down the steps.
As we arrived in the yard we saw our mates standing there without moving and watching the roof.
Suddenly, as we were right in the middle of the yard, we saw a big flame coming out of the roof. The school was in fire.
In fact the main problem was that the fire alarm did not fonction at all.

Examiner's comments:
A weak essay which shows an inability to control the language. The task has not been attempted satisfactorily.

4 MARKS

'Every family should have a computer in the home.' Do you agree?

First of all, I'm trying to explain in few words "What a computer is?"
It's a machine which was invented about sixty years ago. It was invented for helping people in their work, particularly by the technical industry. Bit by bit the computer became indispensable among the ingeniers because of the rapidity of calculate thing and accuracy of the result.
Nowdays in 1989 the computer is not only used by the industries but by everybody who wants a tools that permit him or her to find a lot of information to treat them, to calculate them and so on.
For instance, if you are the manager of an hotel and you want to find out how many people are in the hotel, how many day they are staying, how long they are going to stay. You have push only four buttons on your computer set which is composed of a monitor, a keyboard, the computer itself usually fitted under the monitor and all the things is connected together by cable with plugs systeme. Then you have to insert into the computer a disk which contens your programme.
In conclusion of that, in my opinion, it's a very useful machine for the people who needs it But I don't think every family should have a computer in the home although now every children are taught how to use a computer.

Examiner's comments:
Most of this essay does not attempt to answer the question. The candidate is penalised for irrelevance as well as inaccuracy.

Exam preparation

Students should be given practice in writing compositions on all the different types of topics at the required length (about 150 words) and within the time available (about 45 minutes), and in developing the skill of using language appropriate to, say, a narrative, a formal letter or a speech. In the case of candidates intending to choose in the actual exam one of the topics based on optional reading, suitable practice questions should be devised for them to discuss and write about, based on the current syllabus (published in the Regulations each year).

Paper 3: Use of English (2 hours)

This paper contains a number of exercises which test candidates' active control of English usage and grammatical structures, and a directed writing exercise testing their ability to extract specified information from a text and present it in continuous prose with coherence and the right emphasis.

The exercises include a blank-filling exercise based on a passage (a cloze exercise modified to place emphasis on structural items), a transformation exercise on sentences involving verb forms, prepositions, inversion, comparatives, etc., and other exercises involving word formation, constructing sentences to form a letter, writing part of a dialogue, changing sentences from direct to reported speech or vice versa, and correct choice of structure and vocabulary within associated areas. The range of exercise types is illustrated in *Cambridge First Certificate Practice 4*.

For the final exercise candidates study a text, often containing an illustration, map or diagram, from which they extract the required information. This information is then rewritten in the spaces provided on the answer sheet. These spaces determine the way in which each part of the answer is written as well as its content by, for example, giving the first words of each paragraph that candidates have to complete. This question is in effect a composition exercise depending on information retrieval with a realistic background, standard to all candidates and thus offsetting the open choice of topic in Paper 2.

Marking

The maximum possible mark for Paper 3 may vary between 75 and 90 (later scaled down to a weighted total of 40), with the directed exercise carrying 15 to 20 marks. The latter is given one or more impression marks, along the lines indicated, and attention is given to coverage of relevant points, coherent linking and accuracy of language; an appropriate amount of direct quotation from the text is allowed. Detailed mark schemes are given in this book for each of the five Use of English papers.

Exam preparation

It should be noted that many of the exercises in Paper 3 have more value as testing devices than as classroom exercises. Too much emphasis on such exercises in class may not increase students' language awareness or communicative skills. In particular, the modified cloze test (Question 1) should not be over-practised in class.

In preparing for the directed writing exercise, students should be given practice in extracting information from a variety of different texts and presenting it as two or more paragraphs in their own words.

Paper 4: Listening Comprehension (20 to 30 minutes)

In this paper a cassette recording is played to candidates and they record their answers to a series of questions while they listen. Candidates listen to three or four authentic or simulated-authentic texts, complete with all necessary spoken instructions; each text is normally heard twice on the cassette. The texts include broadcasts, conversations, discussions, announcements and telephone calls. As far as possible, these avoid culture bias and provide a fair test of listening comprehension as a basic skill. The questions include reordering or matching information, labelling and blank-filling, as well as multiple-choice and true/false questions. The questions test candidates' ability to extract information from the texts, to interpret the speakers' attitudes or intentions and to recognise the meaning of stress and intonation patterns.

NB Candidates record their answers to Paper 4 on the question paper initially. At the end of the test they are given five minutes to transfer their answers to a separate answer sheet, an example of which can be found at the back of the Student's Book.

Marking

The final total of 20 marks (which involves the adjustment of raw scores to allow for appropriate weighting parity between test versions and to offset the guessing factor in multiple-choice or true/false questions) gives, together with Paper 5, one third of the total marks in the exam. A complete mark scheme is given in this book for each of the five Listening Comprehension papers.

Exam preparation

Students should become accustomed to the form and tempo of the recordings used in the examination. In particular, they should be exposed to recordings of speakers using unsimplified English, spoken at a natural speed. They should realise that understanding spoken English involves extracting the main points of information from a text and does not necessarily depend on understanding every word that is spoken. Classroom practice using task-based exercises is recommended.

This Teacher's Book contains transcripts of the recordings used in *Cambridge First Certificate Examination Practice 4*. These are included only to help teachers handle the tests confidently and see what each piece is about and how long it lasts. The transcripts should *not* be used to help students to 'spot the answers' to the questions. Many questions depend on interpreting what is heard on the tape, including the stress and intonation of the speakers, which cannot be shown in a transcript.

Note: The recordings of the two cassettes that accompany *Cambridge First Certificate Examination Practice 4* follow the format of the exam exactly. Each text is heard twice with pauses before and after each hearing, during which students can read through the questions or task and write down their answers. There are also full spoken instructions on the cassettes.

Paper 5: Interview (15 to 20 minutes)

The Interview consists of a theme-based conversation between the candidate and the examiner, or in the case of group Interviews, among the candidates with occasional intervention by the examiner. Prompt material consisting of photographs, short passages, authentic texts and problem-solving activities are used to stimulate and guide the discussion. This form of syllabus incorporates developments made over a long period, notably the changes of 1984 which included increased weighting for the Interview, a change of format and an increased time allowance.

The present format emphasises discussion and communicative activities. Candidates are assessed over all the tasks set by marking scales related to six specific performance areas (see marking section on pages 10–12).

Provision is made for centres to opt for the Interview to be taken in the usual candidate/ examiner format or in pairs or in groups of three candidates. The added realism of a pair/group Interview is recommended, but organisational difficulties may make it impracticable for some centres and it is therefore treated as an option. (Instructions will be issued by each centre accordingly.) The increased amount of 'candidate talking time' generated and reduction in 'examiner talking time' mean that pair/group Interviews can be accomplished relatively quickly and do not need to take proportionately longer than an examiner/candidate Interview. Two examiners are required for a group Interview, however, so that one examiner may concentrate on ensuring equal turn-taking, whilst the other functions as assessor only.

Procedure

The examiner's material consists of a number of 'packages' or theme-based sets of photographs and other prompts from which the complete Interview is conducted. The photographs have sets of suggested questions and follow-up topics, not all of which need be used. The conversation should move from specific commentary on the situation shown in the picture to associated themes, with the candidate encouraged to speak freely. Emphasis on the factual aspects of the photographs and questions about, for example, what is visible in the background, are avoided. It should be remembered that it is the candidates' language skills that are being tested, not their personality, intelligence or knowledge of the world.

Candidates are then referred to one or more of the passages and asked to comment on them and/or to link the themes of the passages to the photographs where appropriate. Reading aloud of the passages is **not** required.

The Interview is completed either by a discussion of a piece of authentic material, for example, a leaflet, advertisement, extract from a newspaper or magazine, *and/or* a communicative activity using a variety of visual and verbal stimuli. The range of activities includes participation in a role-playing exercise, finding out information, rank-ordering, giving and exchanging opinions, and problem-solving discussion. There is often an 'information gap' between the participants, leading to a realistic exchange of information and ideas between candidates (where the test is taken as a pair/group) or between candidate and examiner.

The passages and activity prompts include some related to the optional background reading (see *Paper 2: Composition*). The background-text format is similar to that of the general theme-based material.

Cambridge First Certificate Examination Practice 4 contains five sample 'packages' of oral examiner's material (and two optional reading-based 'packages'), which demonstrate the variety of passages and activity prompts used in the examination. Teachers may wish to prepare additional material (photographs, passages, realia) from other sources within the theme of each package to provide students with actual rather than copied material.

Marking

Candidates are marked by impression on different aspects of their spoken English throughout the Interview, as shown in the scales given below. The 'raw' maximum of 30 is scaled to a final total of 40.

1 Fluency

5	Virtually native-speaker speed and rhythm in everyday contexts though there may be some hesitation when speaking on more abstract topics.
4	In everyday contexts speaks with minimal hesitation. Hesitation when discussing abstract topics does not demand unreasonable patience of the listener.
3	Does not hesitate unreasonably in everyday contexts though may experience some difficulty with more abstract topics.
2	Unacceptable hesitation even in everyday contexts.
1	Speech very disconnected.
0	Not capable of connected speech.

2 Grammatical accuracy

5	Few if any errors over a wide range of structures, including tenses, prepositions etc. Completely sufficient to deal with everyday contexts and more than adequate for abstract topics.
4	Basic structures sound though more difficult structures may sometimes be inaccurate.
3	Basic structures sufficiently controlled to deal adequately with everyday contexts though difficulty experienced with more complex structures.
2	Basic structures often inaccurate in everyday contexts. More complex structures rarely attempted or grossly inaccurate.
1	Gross distortion of basic structures.
0	No awareness of basic grammatical functions.

3 Pronunciation: Sentences

5	Near-native stress-timing, rhythm, and placing of stress, intonation patterns and range of pitch within sentence, natural linking of phrases.
4	Good stress-timing, rhythm, placing of stress, intonation etc. so that in spite of sounding foreign, speech is easily understood.
3	Stress-timing, rhythm, placing of stress, intonation etc. noticeably foreign but can mostly be understood.
2	Unacceptably foreign speech patterns predominate, with incorrect phrasing impeding interpretation. Often difficult to understand.
1	Stress and intonation so foreign that little is comprehensible.
0	Not intelligible, through faulty stress and intonation.

4 Pronunciation: Individual sounds

5   All individual sounds virtually as a native-speaker.

4   Individual sounds sufficiently well pronounced for clear and easy understanding.

3   Sounds sufficiently correct for broad understanding.

2   Poor pronunciation of individual sounds.

1   Pronunciation so poor that it represents only a crude approximation to English sounds.

0   Unintelligible.

5 Interactive communication

5   Wholly effective at communicating in everyday contexts. Largely effective in communicating on more abstract topics.

4   Communicates effectively in everyday contexts but lapses sometimes when dealing with more abstract topics.

3   Communicates adequately in everyday contexts but experiences some difficulty in discussing more abstract topics.

2   Experiences difficulty in communicating even in everyday contexts.

1   Rarely able to communicate even at a basic level.

0   Communicates nothing.

6 Vocabulary resource

5   Wide and appropriate range of vocabulary for everyday tasks and rarely searching for vocabulary when discussing more abstract topics.

4   Shows few gaps in vocabulary for everyday tasks though more abstract topics reveal weaknesses.

3   Vocabulary adequate for everyday tasks though may experience difficulty when discussing more abstract topics.

2   Vocabulary often insufficient to accomplish even everyday tasks.

1   Severe lack of vocabulary makes it almost impossible to communicate.

0   Vocabulary too slight for even minimal communication.

Exam preparation

Students should be encouraged at all times to do more than just 'answer questions' and to participate actively in a variety of communicative activities and discussions. Talking together in groups or in pairs is particularly valuable. Students may need special training in quick absorption of the relevant discussion content of passages and a variety of authentic material without attempting to puzzle out every word or background reference.

Note: The Student's Book of *Cambridge First Certificate Examination Practice 4* contains a selection of examination material (photographs, passages and prompts for communicative activities) printed separately at the end of the book. This material is given in the Teacher's Book as Paper 5 in each practice test. Each Interview paper is theme-related and has instructions for use. One 'package' based on a sample set text is included, after the theme-based Interview Exercises. Teachers' instructions for this are given on pages 82–84.

Practice Test 1

Paper 1: Reading Comprehension (1 hour)

Section A   Give one mark for each correct answer.

1 B	6 B	11 B	16 B	21 D
2 A	7 D	12 C	17 A	22 A
3 C	8 B	13 A	18 B	23 A
4 D	9 C	14 B	19 C	24 C
5 A	10 D	15 D	20 C	25 B

Section B   Give two marks for each correct answer.

26 A	31 B	36 C
27 D	32 C	37 A
28 B	33 C	38 C
29 A	34 C	39 C
30 B	35 B	40 B

Total: 55

Paper 2: Composition (1½ hours)

Give each composition a mark out of 20, according to the scale below. Compositions of less than 120 words should lose marks. If necessary, look at the sample compositions on pages 4–7 for further guidance on the standards required at each grade in the mark scheme.

	Language	*Task*
18–20	Natural English with minimal errors.	Full realisation of task.
16–17	More than a collection of simple sentences, with good vocabulary and structures. Some occasional lapses.	
11–15	Sufficient naturalness of English and not many errors.	Simple but accurate realisation of the task.
8–10	Communication established despite some errors.	Task reasonably attempted.
5–7	Lack of control/frequent basic errors.	Task only partly realised (by neglect of the rubric).
1–4	Incoherence.	Gross irrelevance, and/or too short for language assessment.

Total: 40

Paper 3: Use of English (2 hours)

A complete mark scheme is given for each question. The 'raw' total of 86 for this paper would be adjusted to a mark out of 40 in the exam itself. Candidates passing the examination as a whole would be expected to score about 60% of the total marks.

Question 1   Give one mark for each correct answer.

1 with	11 but/However/Yet/Unfortunately/Strangely/Incredibly/Surprisingly
2 while/whilst	(capital letters essential where specified)
3 not	12 asked/enquired/inquired
4 back	13 with
5 them	14 in/on/beside/behind
6 less	15 trying
7 believe	16 heard/noticed
8 windows	17 got/jumped/stepped/sprang/leapt
9 their/just	18 were/found/saw/sat/crouched/knelt/lay
10 to/round	19 it
	20 almost/nearly/practically/just/simply

Total: 20

Question 2

Give one mark for each word or phrase between the vertical lines, or two marks where shown. (Ignore the words printed in italics.)

a)   *Joan eats very little because* | s/he does not want | to put on weight.
| s/he does not wish | get fat.
| | grow fat.
| | become fat. |

OR *Joan eats very little because* | s/he wants to avoid | putting on weight.
| s/he wishes to avoid | getting fat.
| s/he is afraid of | growing fat.
| s/he is frightened of | becoming fat. |
| s/he is scared of |
| s/he is worried about |
| s/he is anxious about |
| s/he is concerned about |

b) *When the goods* | arrive in/at the shop, they | *are inspected carefully.*
| have arrived in/at the shop, they |
| reach the shop, they |
| have reached the shop, they |
| get to the shop, they |
| have got to the shop, they |
| are delivered to/at the shop, they |
| have been delivered to/at the shop, they | (2 marks)

Practice Test 1

c) *Laurence last*	saw his sister	when she left for Japan.
		before she went to Japan.
		on her departure for Japan.
		before her departure for Japan.

d) *Peter said, "I*	am not feeling well."
	don't feel well."
	am feeling sick."
	feel sick."
	unwell."
	ill."

e) *If*	John/he did not eat so many chips	he would not be (so) fat.
	John/he ate fewer chips	as fat as he is.
	John/he ate less chips	he would be less fat.
		thinner.
		slimmer.

| f) *The doctor advised* | Mr Roberts | to take more exercise | if he wanted to lose weight. |
| | him | to do more exercise | (in order/so as) to lose weight. |

g) *Jane is*	interested in collecting	*dolls from foreign countries.*
	keen on	
	fond of	(2 marks)

OR *Jane is*	someone (who/that is)	interested in collecting	*dolls from foreign countries.*
	somebody		
	a girl		

h) *George used*	to be much	more energetic (than he is now/at present).
	far	
	a lot	
	considerably	
	a great deal	

OR *George used*	to have much	more energy (than he does now/at present).
	far	
	a lot	
	considerably	
	a great deal	

i) *Unless*	Joe/he changes his ways,	*he will end up in prison.*
	mends his ways,	
	reforms	(2 marks)

Total: 18

Question 3   Give one mark for each correct answer.

a) book/reserve/make sure of
b) menu
c) pudding/dessert/sweet/afters
d) course
e) tip/gratuity

Total: 5

Question 4   Give one mark for each correct answer.

a) give way
b) give in
c) give up
d) give back
e) give it away/it to charity

Total: 5

Question 5

There is a possible total of three marks for each answer.
For three marks an answer must be totally correct, including spelling.
Give two marks for a satisfactory answer with minor errors.
Give one mark for answers that communicate the right meaning but have serious errors, e.g. in the question form or in tenses.

Examples of correct answers (others are possible):
1 *What* subjects did you study there?
2 *And why* did you decide to study these particular subjects?
3 *And can you* speak any other languages?
4 *Where* did you have Spanish lessons?
5 *Have* you ever been to/visited Japan?
6 *What* do you like doing in your free time?

Total: 18

Question 6

This part of the paper is intended to test the candidate's ability to select specified information and present it in continuous form, with coherence and the right emphasis. The task is one of making out a plausible case in the light of the given data and expressing relevant points with clarity, conciseness and a reasonable degree of fluency.

   Give an impression mark of 0–5 for each paragraph. Good answers should combine valid, well-supported reasons with maturity of expression – grammatical accuracy, good linking, a reasonable vocabulary range and conciseness. A maximum of 5 may be awarded to answers with very minor errors, e.g. spelling or prepositions. Penalise extensive "lifting" and serious grammatical errors.

Total: 20

Paper 4: Listening Comprehension (about 30 minutes)

Part one: Life insurance

		Score
1	Brown	1
2	12	½
3	secretary	1
4	18 months ago	1
5	No	½
6	10 a day	1
7	wine	1
8	No	½
9	ski-ing	1

Total: 7½ marks

Part two: Botswana

		Score
10	C	1
11	D	1
12	A	1
13	D	1

Total: 4 marks

Part three: Station announcements

		Score
14	7	½
15	11	½
16	11.45	½
17	Connections	1
18	Cambridge	1

Total: 3½ marks

Part four: Community centre

Score

19	dance	√	½
20	swimming		½
21	boxing		½
22	football	√	½
23	weight training	√	½
24	volleyball		½
25	karate & kung fu	√	½
26	brass band		½
27	drama	√	½
28	table tennis	√	½

Total: 5 marks

Total marks: 20

Transcript

Cambridge First Certificate in English.
Test Number 1
You will be given a question paper and separate answer sheet for First Certificate Test 1. There are four parts to the test and each part will be heard twice. During the test, there will be pauses before each part to allow you to look through the questions, and other pauses to let you think about your answers. At the end of every pause you will hear this sound.

tone

You should write your answers on the question paper. You will have five minutes at the end to transfer your answers to the separate answer sheet.
    The tape will now be stopped while question papers are given out. You must ask any questions now, as you will not be allowed to speak during the test.

pause

Part one
You will hear a woman asking for details about life insurance. Fill in the missing information in the spaces numbered 1 to 9 on the Personal Statement below.

pause

tone

LIFE INSURANCE

Man: Good morning, madam, can I help you?
Woman: I'd like some details about Life Insurance, please.

Man: Yes, I shall have to take some personal details and I can give you a quote or send it through the post.
Woman: Well, if you send it through the post that'll be easier, I think.
Man: Right . . . well, if you haven't any objection perhaps we could complete this statement (*Yes that's fine.*) and then I can send it off to our brokers in London. Your name?
Woman: Elizabeth Brown. (*Is that Miss or Mrs?*) um, Miss. (*Yes, all right.*)
Man: And where were you born? (*Birmingham.*) And your date of birth? (*17.12.1960*) . . . 12.60. So you'll be, er, let's see, um, 25 next birthday? (*That's right, yeah.*) And your job or profession? (*Um, I'm a secretary.*) That's a full-time job? (*Yes.*) And your address?
Woman: Number 3, Johnstone Street, St. Pauls, Bristol.
Man: Does it have a postcode?
Woman: I can't remember it at the moment.
Man: Doesn't matter, it's not important. Now, telephone number . . .
Woman: Er, yes, Bristol 22041.
Man: Right, now, the next set of details we have to do for medical purposes (*right*) . . . your height?
Woman: 1 metre 63.
Man: Do you know your weight approximately?
Woman: 58 kilos.
Man: I see, um, now, have you a doctor in Bristol?
Woman: Um, no, my doctor . . . well I can't remember if I've changed my doctor because I've only moved to Bristol recently. I'd have to check that out for you. I'm really not sure about that.
Man: Can you remember when you last consulted a doctor?
Woman: About 18 months ago.
Man: I see and what was that for? Anything serious?
Woman: I had my appendix out.
Man: Appendix . . . I see, right . . . are you on a diet or any particular treatment or taking any pills or drugs? (*No.*) Right. The following questions. Do you smoke? (*Yes.*) I see, and how much do you smoke? (*About ten a day.*) Do you drink?
Woman: How do you mean?
Man: Well do you regularly for example have two or three pints of beer a day or a couple of gin and tonics?
Woman: Maybe a couple of times a week I go out for a drink. I don't drink more than a couple of glasses of wine.
Man: I see – now your family . . . your family, you have parents? (*Yes, I do.*) Are they still alive? (*Yes, they are.*) Right, brothers and sisters? (*Yes.*) And they're still alive? (*Yes.*) And do you intend to journey abroad and that means fairly frequently not just for holidays?
Woman: No, I would only go for holidays.
Man: Right. Do you take part in any dangerous sports such as mountaineering or diving or . . .?
Woman: I go ski-ing.
Man: Ah, and is that fairly regularly?
Woman: Only in winter, once a year.
Man: Right, I'll just make a note of that. Now if you'd like to sign where it says signature and today's date then we can get a quote for you in a few days . . .

pause

tone

Now you will hear the piece again. [The piece is repeated.]

pause

That is the end of the first part of the test.

pause

Part two
You will now hear a radio programme about building water tanks in Botswana. For each of the questions 10 to 13 you will see four pictures. Tick one of the boxes A, B, C or D to show which picture gives the best answer to each question.

pause

tone

BOTSWANA

Radio presenter:	And now we turn to another development in Southern Africa. The country this time is Botswana and the particular part of Botswana is the Kalahari Desert, an extremely dry region in which the government now has a scheme to preserve water. Ralph Weaver has been talking to Jack Nickerson, who's been working on it and he suggested to him that although the Kalahari Desert is so dry, there must be some water or there couldn't be any human settlements.
Jack Nickerson:	Yes, what you say is very true. Of course we do get rain in the Kalahari in the summer season, though normally it sinks straight into the ground and is lost. But the Botswana Ministry of Agriculture has developed a scheme whereby they would assist farmers with the construction of underground water tanks. Now this is rainfall run-off water, which can be diverted underground into a thing which resembles a very large bottle, made of brick and plastered up on the inside, and only the neck of the bottle is coming up to the surface.
Ralph Weaver:	And will it store rainwater?
Jack Nickerson:	Yes, and the rainwater wouldn't normally run off the Kalahari sandy surface. But in every agricultural area or settlement in Botswana there's always a floor made of solid mud and earth. And of course the rain that falls on that won't penetrate at all, normally just has to run off the floor and then is lost and wasted. Well, what we've been doing is helping farmers to install these underground tanks. We did the first about a year ago. And very shortly afterwards there was a very good rain. And it was very, very satisfying to see that these tanks really did work and were filled up by the rainfall run-off, which would otherwise have been lost. And that water, which is drawn up from the bottle just as you would draw up water from a well, with a bucket and a rope, is used for human consumption and also the all-important watering of the cattle.
Ralph Weaver:	And the shape of the tank with this narrow neck – is that to stop the water evaporating, being lost?
Jack Nickerson:	No, there can be no evaporation whatsoever because the whole tank is buried under the sand.

21

Ralph Weaver:	And you put a cover over it?
Jack Nickerson:	That's right. And the tank narrows to the top, what you might call the neck of the bottle. And over that we put a lid. It's a lid made very simply of an old tractor wheel with the middle filled in with cement and a handle fixed on. Heavy enough so that no child could move it. Because, of course, these tanks would be very dangerous if anybody fell into them.
Ralph Weaver:	And tanks like these would be fairly simple to build wouldn't they?
Jack Nickerson:	Oh, yes. The farmers themselves have to dig the initial hole, which is quite a big hole and about three men can do the job.
Ralph Weaver:	And the only things you'd need to buy probably would be the cement?
Jack Nickerson:	The cement, yes, and a few pieces of plastic and wire netting. That's just about all there is to it.

pause

tone

Now you will hear the piece again. [The piece is repeated.]

pause

That is the end of the second part of the test.

pause

Part three
You will hear some station announcements about train departures from Birmingham station. Look at the departure board below and fill in the missing information in the spaces numbered 14 to 18.

pause

tone

STATION ANNOUNCEMENTS

Platform alteration. Here is a platform alteration. The train now standing on Platform 7 is the 11.35, calling at all stations to Wolverhampton.
    The train standing at Platform 11 is the 11.38 to Taunton, calling at Cheltenham Spa, Bristol Parkway, Bristol Temple Meads and Taunton. Change at Bristol Temple Meads for Weymouth and Weston. Change at Taunton for Exeter, Torquay, Paignton and Plymouth.
    Train announcement. The 11.45 to Glasgow and Edinburgh will be subject to slight delay due to damage to overhead cable near Blockby.
    Train announcement. The 11.45 to Derby will be slightly delayed leaving Birmingham, awaiting connections.
    The train standing at Platform 4 is the 11.52 to Cambridge. This train contains a restaurant and buffet car services.

pause

tone

Now you will hear the piece again. [The piece is repeated.]

pause

That is the end of the third part of the test.

pause

Part four
You will hear an interview with someone called Michaela, who helps to run a club for young people. For questions 19–28 below, tick the boxes to show which activities organised at the Community Centre are mentioned by Michaela. If the activity is not mentioned, leave the box blank.

pause

tone

COMMUNITY CENTRE

Presenter: A young Trinidadian with charm and initiative has recently set up a community centre in South London, using her own money until the ILEA, the Inner London Education Authority, contributed £1000 for equipment. Michaela Campbell decided to put the empty building, which was once her school, to good use. She set up various workshops and now the Old Paragon school is occupied almost every evening by young local black kids, learning karate, dance and weight training. Michaela, why did you set up the centre?

Michaela: There are a lot of black people in South London that, uh, are not really catered for, black people in the sense that black young people who are gifted in creativity, in dance, in drama, in, uh, wanting to express themselves. The Paragon school was a youth club, but not a very well-run youth club so I decided to come in and I offered the youth warden at the time, I said to him that I can get people to use the premises, he laughed but I knew, you know, I believed in what I said, and now you know we've got two dance groups, we've got a drama group, we've got weight-training, we've got karate, we've got Kung Fu, we've got football, table tennis . . .

Presenter: Michaela, how did you actually finance all of this?

Michaela: I was at college studying fashion, and um I was given a grant each term, about uh £700 . . .

pause

tone

Now you will hear the piece again. [The piece is repeated.]

pause

That is the end of the fourth part of the test.

There will now be a five-minute pause to allow you to check your work and transfer your answers to the separate answer sheet. The question papers and answer sheets will then be collected by your supervisor.

pause

tone

That is the end of the test.

Paper 5: Interview (about 15 minutes)

FAMILY AND FRIENDS

The following sample package of oral examiner's material enables a complete interview to be practised and students' speaking skills to be assessed according to the marking scales given on pages 10–12. The photographs, passages and activities for Practice Test 1 can be found at the back of the Student's Book.

Photographs   (usually about 5 minutes)

Refer the students to one or more of the photographs on pages 101–102 of the Student's Book.

1

2

3

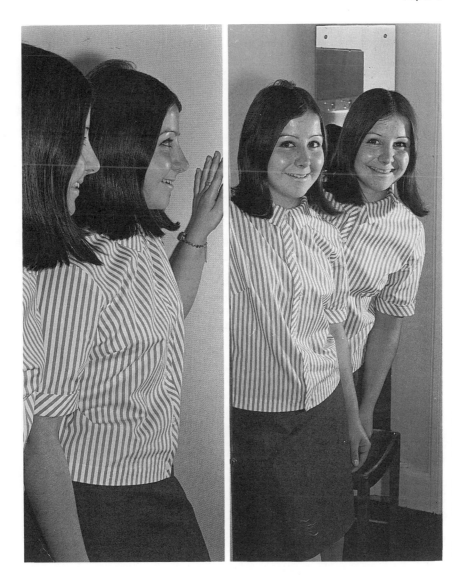

Allow a suitable short interval for study, then open discussion along the lines suggested.
Describe/compare the people; their relationship with each other; the setting.
The conversation should then lead on to an informal discussion of one or more of the following
subjects:

– the advantages and disadvantages of large families
– what it would be like to have a twin
– whether one is closer to friends or family

Questions such as the following may help to lead the conversation in the right direction,
although students should be encouraged to sustain their part in the conversation beyond
simple question-and-answer.

Do you have any brothers or sisters? What are they like?
Do you think it's a good thing to be part of a large family? Why?
Do you have a lot of friends? Are they more important to you than your family?
Would you like to have lots of children one day? Why?
What do you think are the advantages of having a twin?

Passages (usually about 2 minutes)

Refer students to one or more of the passages on page 102 of the Student's Book. Invite the students to try and link the themes of the passages to the photographs. For further discussion you may ask the students to comment on the passages, saying what sort of passages they are. Students should *not* be asked to read a whole passage aloud but may quote from it where this arises naturally during the course of the conversation.

4   Me? I'd hate to have a twin. Just imagine having someone who looked just like you, talked like you and probably dressed like you! How could you feel like your*self* with your double walking around!!

5   Well, I come from a family of seven children and I'm glad because when I was young I had brothers and sisters around to help me. Even if I didn't get along with one there were plenty of others. But we did have some hard times with so many mouths to feed.

6   My best friend and I are even closer than sisters. We do everything together, talk about everything. I can't talk to my own sister at all. But then, she's six years older than me.

Tasks (usually about 5 minutes)

Choose one of the following tasks from Interview Exercises 7, 8 and 9.

7   *Discussion activity* (suitable for an individual, pair or group interview)

Refer students to the list of the qualities we look for in a friend (printed below and on page 000 of the Student's Book).
Invite students to list the three most important qualities they would look for in a friend.
Ask for examples of these qualities and find out which qualities the students think their friends might find in them!

The qualities we look for in a friend
 – a sense of humour
 – loyalty
 – honesty
 – agreeing with everything you say

- hard working
- having the same interests as you
- good looks
- patience
- intelligence
- skill at sports

8

Role play (suitable for pair or group interview)

Refer students to the role play on page 103 of the Student's Book and assign roles A, B and C to students.

Role A   You borrowed your brother's (sister's) cassette player without asking and accidentally broke it. Have a talk with him (her) about it.

Role B   Your brother (sister) borrowed your cassette player without asking and broke it. Have a talk with him (her) about it.

Role C   Your son (daughter) borrowed his (her) brother's (sister's) cassette player without asking and broke it. Have a talk with your children about it.

If time allows you may ask the students what they would do in such a situation and expand the theme of family relationships.

9

Discussion

Refer students to the quotations below and on page 103 of the Student's Book.

An only child is a lonely child.

Blood is thicker than water.

It's better to have one really good friend than lots of acquaintances.

Invite the students to comment on one or all of these statements and to say how far they agree with them.

Practice Test 2

Paper 1: Reading Comprehension (1 hour)

Section A   Give one mark for each correct answer.

1 C	6 C	11 A	16 D	21 D
2 B	7 A	12 B	17 B	22 B
3 A	8 B	13 B	18 A	23 A
4 A	9 C	14 D	19 C	24 B
5 D	10 C	15 D	20 A	25 A

Section B   Give two marks for each correct answer.

26 C	31 B	36 C
27 C	32 D	37 C
28 A	33 A	38 B
29 B	34 C	39 D
30 C	35 B	40 A

Total: 55

Paper 2: Composition (1½ hours)

See pages 3–7 for mark scheme and sample compositions.

Paper 3: Use of English (2 hours)

A complete mark scheme is given for each question. The 'raw' total of 95 for this paper would be adjusted to a mark out of 40 in the exam itself. Candidates passing the examination as a whole would be expected to score about 60% of the total marks.

Question 1   Give one mark for each correct answer.

1 was
2 as
3 Neither
4 little
5 so
6 between
7 by/through/from/for
8 most/especially/particularly/passionately/best/doing
9 When
10 one
11 where
12 made/insisted/demanded
13 before/until/till
14 him/Chaplin/it/this
15 being
16 that/which
17 money/cash
18 at
19 There
20 birth/origin(s)/childhood/
infancy/babyhood

Total: 20

Question 2

Give one mark for each word or phrase between the vertical lines, or two marks where shown. (Ignore the words printed in italics.)

a) *Tim wondered* | if / whether | he would (ever) find / he would (ever) get / he would (ever) obtain / he was (ever) going to find | *a job.*

b) *In case* | you (should) get lost *in those mountains,*

| you should take / you ought to take / you had better take / I advise you to take / I suggest/recommend (that) you (should) take / I suggest/recommend your taking | *a map.*

c) *A thermometer is* | something which is / a thing which is | (used) for measuring temperature. / (used) to measure temperature. |

OR *A thermometer is* | something which/that / a thing which/that | measures temperature.

d) *You didn't* | forget to post / fail to (remember to) post *the letter,* | did you? |

e) *I had* | the (washing) machine fixed / my (washing) machine mended / repaired | by Mr Dryden. / by him. |

OR *I had* | Mr Dryden mend the (washing) machine for me. | (2 marks)

f) *No one* | in the class is / in her class is | as tall as Pat (is). / so tall as Pat (is). / taller than Pat (is). |

g) *You can only* | get (the) 40%/the discount / receive (the) 40%/the discount / have (the) 40%/the discount / obtain (the) 40%/the discount / secure (the) 40%/the discount | if you buy / by buying |

all twelve books at the same time.

h) | *Paul apologised* | for | having given Susan/her the wrong number.
giving Susan/her the wrong number.

OR *Paul apologised* | to Susan for | giving (her) the wrong number.

i) | *Samuel has* | kept a diary
been keeping a diary | for (the last) five years.
for (the last) 5 years.
since 1983.

j) | *I'd rather* | you | did not smoke
didn't smoke | *in the kitchen.*

Total: 20

Question 3   Give one mark for each correct answer.

a) out of doors
b) out of work
c) out of sight
d) out of order/service
e) out of date

Total: 5

Question 4   Give one mark for each correct answer.

a) vacancy
b) sack/push/boot
c) post/position
d) employ/hire/recruit
e) promotion/advancement/getting/rising/advancing/moving

Total: 5

Question 5

Give one mark for each word or phrase between the vertical lines, or two marks where shown.
(Ignore the words printed in italics.)

a) *I* | stayed | in / at | *your hotel* | from | *24 April* | to / until / till | *30 April* | in | *room 415.*

b) *On* | arriving / my arrival | *(back) home, I* | realised (that) | *I* | had left | a *book* / my

in my / the *room.*

c) *I* | wonder / was wondering / am wondering | if / whether | *it* | has been found / had been found | and / or | handed *in.*

d) *It* | is / was | a | *small, hardback book* | with a / in a | *blue cover* | (and is) called |

'Gallions Reach' | (written) by | *H.M. Tomlinson.*

e) *I* | am | *very anxious* | to | *get* | the / this / my | *book back because it* | is | *now*

out of print and it | is / would be / will be | *difficult* | to | *find* | in | *bookshops.*

f) *Also,* | the book was given / this | *to me* | by the | *author,* | whose / and his |

signature | is | on the / inside the | *front cover.*

g) *I* | enclose | *a* | *cheque* | for | *£1.50* | to | | *cover*
am enclosing | | | | | | which will
have enclosed | | | | | | which would

the | *cost* | of posting it back | to | *me.*
any

h) *If, unfortunately, you* | do not | *find the book, please return*
cannot
are unable to

(me) the cheque.
the cheque (to me).

Total: 41: reduce to 21

Question 6

This part of the paper is intended to test the candidate's ability to extract specified information and present it in continuous form. The task is one of making out a plausible case in the light of the given data and expressing relevant points with clarity, conciseness and a reasonable degree of fluency.

Each paragraph is marked out of 12: 6 marks for content and 6 marks for expression.

Total: 24

Paper 4: Listening Comprehension (about 30 minutes)

Part one: Police file

	Score
1 A	1
2 C	1
3 A	1
4 B	1
5 D	1

Total: 5 marks

Part two: Personnel interview

		Score
6	personal assistant/p.a.	1
7	(nearly) 5 years/4	1
8	clerk	1
9	receptionist	1
10	conferences	1
11	French	1

Total: 6 marks

Part three: Ford Fiesta

		Score
12	Ford Fiesta/car	1
13	win	1
14	25/twenty-five pence	1
15	6/six	1
16	£4,500	1

Total: 5 marks

Part four: Travel information

		Score
17	M1	1
	M6	1
18	rail services	1
19	limited accommodation available	1
	crowded roads to coastal ports	1
	strike action	1

Total: 6 marks

Total marks: 22

Transcript

Cambridge First Certificate in English.
Test Number 2
You will be given a question paper and separate answer sheet for First Certificate Test 2. There are four parts to the test and each part will be heard twice. During the test, there will be pauses before each part to allow you to look through the questions, and other pauses to let you think about your answers. At the end of every pause you will hear this sound.

tone

You should write your answers on the question paper. You will have five minutes at the end to transfer your answers to the separate answer sheet.

The tape will now be stopped while question papers are given out. You must ask any questions now, as you will not be allowed to speak during the test.

pause

Part one
You will hear part of a radio programme in which listeners are asked to help the police with a crime at Wellington Mews. For each of the questions 1 to 5, tick one of the boxes to show which is the correct answer.

pause

tone

POLICE FILE

Welcome to another edition of Police File, the programme where you the listeners are asked to help us, the police, in solving recently committed crimes.

This week we report on a burglary which occurred in the Central London area earlier this week.

On the night of Tuesday 13th March a house in Wellington Mews, Mayfair was broken into and several valuable items were stolen. Among these items were two unusual pieces of antique silver and the police have issued the following descriptions.

The first is a large bowl, hallmarked and engraved with the maker's name in 1797. The bowl is 30 cms in diameter and about 22 cms deep, it has two ornate handles and a very distinctive floral design round the side.

The second item is a silver tray which has been in the owner's family for over 200 years. It's easily recognized because of its unusual six-sided shape and the initials WM which appear in the centre. The edge of the tray also bears a fine pattern.

The thief was disturbed by the return of the owner's housekeeper who saw a man escaping through the garden at the back of the house. The man is described as tall and slim, in his twenties and is thought to have a beard. At the time he was wearing jeans and a dark jacket and was carrying what looked like a shopping bag. The police are particularly interested in hearing from anyone who may have seen the man answering this description in the vicinity at the time or who can give further information about a dark van seen parked outside the house earlier that evening.

pause

tone
Now you will hear the piece again. [The piece is repeated.]

pause

That is the end of the first part of the test.

pause

Part two
You will now hear a man being interviewed for a job. As you listen to the conversation, complete the interview form by filling in the spaces numbered 6 to 11.

pause

tone

PERSONNEL INTERVIEW

Mrs Hardwood: Ah good morning Mr . . .?

Mr Allan: Good morning Miss Hardwood.

Mrs Hardwood: Mrs Hardwood.

Mr Allan: Oh, sorry.

Mrs Hardwood: Mr Michael Allan (*that's right yes*) do have a seat please (*thank you*). Ah now let's see, you've come for the job as my personal assistant.

Mr Allan: Yes, yes I have.

Mrs Hardwood: I see, now I've got your application form here but I would just like to go through it for a moment (*yes certainly*) now I see you've been the public relations officer at Hargreaves for how long is it . . .?

Mr Allan: In fact I've been there for four years, nearly five years actually.

Mrs Hardwood: I see right um and what did you do before you were at Hargreaves?

Mr Allan: Well before that I was just a clerk, I hadn't learnt shorthand then, but I thought it would be good if I qualified and learned shorthand, so before that I was just a clerk in another company.

Mrs Hardwood: I see Mr Allan, well of course the job here does call for a great deal more than shorthand and typing (*oh yes I do understand that*) I'm sure you realize that, now do you speak any foreign languages?

Mr Allan: Yes, I do actually. I speak French, and in fact I thought it would be very important for me to keep it up and I'm going to night school in French so it's at a reasonable level at the moment.

Mrs Hardwood: Oh I see very good right, the reason I ask that sort of question is that if you were to get the job then you would, I would expect you to act on your own quite a bit and for instance next week I've got representatives from four European countries coming here for a conference, and I'd expect you to make all the arrangements for that, feeding them and so on. Just give me some idea how you would set about that, could you?

Mr Allan: Well it certainly sounds very demanding, but um I think actually my experience as a receptionist, I forgot to say to you that I had, when I was a clerk been working as a receptionist . . .

Mrs Hardwood: I see, where was that?

Mr Allan: Well that was at the new hotel down in George Street (*ah yes, yes*) it was only in the evening part time just to increase my income a bit and just for the experience so I am used to organizing . . .

Mrs Hardwood: Did you organize conferences?

Mr Allan: Yes I did, so I think I'd feel happy organizing your conference. Would I have to do hotel bookings and actually arrange the whole running of the conference . . .?

pause

tone

Now you will hear the piece again. [The piece is repeated.]

pause

That is the end of the second part of the test.

pause

Part three
You will hear a man trying to get people to enter a competition to win a prize. Look at the advertisement about the competition and fill in the missing information in the spaces numbered 12 to 16.

pause

tone

FORD FIESTA

. . . he must be mad I hear you all cry in amazement! Now ladies and gents, it is true, a man did win the car yesterday, it's your turn to win the car today, come on, come on, the man in Wells won yesterday, come forward, don't stand back there, come on, have a go, no, the catch is 25 pence, 25 pence to win a four and a half thousand pounds motor car.
Now you've read about it in the paper, you've seen it on the telly, come on, it's your turn to win this car today, for just 25 pence.
(*What kind of car is it?*) It's a red Ford Fiesta lady, and it could be yours for 25 pence. Now come on, it was done yesterday, let's see if it can be done today . . . (*Let's see the car!*) Ah, the car's right round the back here. Right round the back. Ah, would I pull the wool over your eyes, would I? Course I wouldn't. Now, 25 pence for four and a half thousand pounds worth of motor car . . . and . . . we had a winner yesterday, his name was Alan Jones and when he drove away he thought himself a very lucky man. Now come on, come on lady . . . Let that lady through, let that lady through, have a go, one roll on the dice my dear and it could be yours, go on. Ah, unlucky . . . quickly now, we've got five sixes turned up, it's going in closer now . . . we want six sixes, a brand new car, four and a half thousand pounds worth . . .

pause

tone
Now you will hear the piece again. [The piece is repeated.]

pause

That is the end of the third part of the test.

Part Four
You will hear some recorded travel information from the BBC Motoring and Travel Unit. For each of the questions 17 to 19, tick one or more boxes to show the correct answers. Use the map on p. 42 to help you.

pause

tone

TRAVEL INFORMATION

Here's the British Telecom travel bulletin prepared by the BBC Motoring and Travel Unit. This bulletin is valid until 07.00 hours tomorrow.
All domestic services are operating normally this weekend but airports will be very crowded today as many holiday-makers are returning home. Roads are likely to be very busy because of the Bank Holiday. Motorways continue to be affected by the summer repair programme and roadworks on the M1 between junctions 15 and 16 and a five mile stretch of

the M6 north of Birmingham are causing considerable delays.

Engineering works are affecting rail services. Delays of up to one hour can be expected on some routes in the southern region and on others, trains have been replaced by buses and so rail travellers are advised to allow extra time for their journeys. However trains from Reading to Gatwick are running normally as are underground services to Heathrow. Further details are available on BBC local radio.

And now here is the British Telecom travel bulletin for sea travellers. Sea crossings should be comfortable again today as weather conditions in the Channel and North Sea are good. All ferry services are operating normally except the Felixstowe–Zeebrugge which continues to be affected by strikes. Limited space is still available on most crossings but prospective passengers with cars are advised to telephone their local agency before setting out. Roads to the coast are very busy, so allow extra time for the journey. Rail travellers will also have problems because of engineering works and certain services in the southern region are subject to cancellation and delays.

pause

tone
Now you will hear the piece again. [The piece is repeated.]

pause

That is the end of the fourth part of the test.

There will now be a five-minute pause to allow you to check your work and transfer your answers to the separate answer sheet. The question papers and answer sheets will then be collected by your supervisor.

pause

tone
That is the end of the test.

Paper 5: Interview (about 15 minutes)

THE SEA

The following sample package of oral examiner's material enables a complete interview to be practised and students' speaking skills to be assessed according to the marking scales given on pages 10–12. The photographs, passages and activities for Practice Test 2 can be found at the back of the Student's Book.

Photographs   (usually about 5 minutes)

Refer students to one or more of the photographs on pages 104–105 of the Student's Book.

10

11

12

Allow a suitable short interval for study, then open discussion along the lines suggested. Describe/compare the people; the setting and the weather; the activity.

The conversation should then lead on to an informal discussion of one or more of the following subjects:

- sports activities associated with the sea
- what the sea can provide
- the dangers of the sea

Questions such as the following may help to lead the conversation in the right direction, although students should be encouraged to sustain their part in the conversation beyond simple question-and-answer.

Do you like the sea? Why?
What kind of sports can be practised on the sea?
What kind of work is associated with the sea?
Do you think the sea is dangerous? Why?
Could you live off the sea?

Passages   (usually about 2 minutes)

Refer students to one or more of the passages on page 105 of the Student's Book. Invite students to try and link the themes of the passages to the photographs. For further discussion you may ask the students to comment on the passages, saying what sort of passages they are. Students should *not* be asked to read a whole passage aloud but may quote from it where this arises naturally during the course of the conversation.

13   That's something I've always wanted to try. It looks so easy when you watch someone doing it, but I guess you need a pretty good sense of balance.

14   Once out on the open sea the men began to relax and enjoy it. There was just enough breeze to get up a good speed but not enough to make the sea too rough. The sun shone down out of a cloudless blue sky. It was a perfect day for sailing.

15   Here she comes now! Thank goodness the supplies will be here before the winter. Another week or so and no ships will get in or out of here.

Tasks   (usually about 5 minutes)

Choose one or both of the following tasks from Interview Exercises 16 and 17.

16   *Discussion*

Invite students to discuss what they imagine to be the good and bad points of the following:

being a fisherman   living by the sea
being a deep-sea diver   a holiday by the sea

39

being a beach lifeguard   going on a long cruise
being in the navy

It is not necessary to cover *all* the items in the list.
It may be helpful to ask students to compare the items on the list with contrasting ones e

How do you think being a beach lifeguard would compare with working in an office?
What are the differences between living by the sea and living in a city or in the countr

17 *Activity*

Invite students to imagine that they love the sea. Refer them to the free holiday
announcement below and on page 106 of the Student's Book, and outline the
following situation:

You have won first prize in a competition. The prize is a free holiday on the sea
for four people, for four weeks, anywhere in the world.

Discuss and decide

– what kind of holiday you would choose (relaxing, active, sports)
– who you would take with you and why
– where you would go
– what you would take with you (e.g. food, radio, maps, clothes etc.)
– how you would spend your time.

NB   If the students appear to dislike the sea, suggest an alternative prize of a
£1,000 travel voucher. Ask similar questions to those related to the sea holidays.

Practice Test 3

Paper 1: Reading Comprehension (1 hour)

Section A Give one mark for each correct answer.

1 C	6 D	11 B	16 C	21 C
2 C	7 A	12 B	17 D	22 D
3 C	8 A	13 D	18 D	23 A
4 A	9 B	14 A	19 B	24 C
5 B	10 C	15 C	20 C	25 B

Section B Give two marks for each correct answer.

26 D	31 C	36 D
27 A	32 D	37 D
28 B	33 C	38 D
29 C	34 B	39 A
30 A	35 B	40 B

Total: 55

Paper 2: Composition (1½ hours)

See pages 3–7 for mark scheme and sample compositions.

Paper 3: Use of English (2 hours)

A complete mark scheme is given for each question. The 'raw' total of 89 for this paper would be adjusted to a mark out of 40 in the exam itself. Candidates passing the examination as a whole would be expected to score about 60% of the total marks.

Question 1 Give one mark for each correct answer.

1 Though/Although
2 a
3 before
4 to
5 was
6 pictures/film/footage/reports/shots/coverage
7 would/should/must
8 singers/stars/musicians/groups/personalities/bands
9 use/utilise
10 it/this
11 made/raised
12 which
13 more
14 other
15 being/getting
16 shown/broadcast/live
17 been
18 or
19 watching/viewing
20 did

Total: 20

Question 2

Give one mark for each word or phrase between the vertical lines, or two marks where shown. (Ignore the words printed in italics.)

a) *Sally* | was given a microcomputer | for her birthday by her parents.
                                          by her parents for her birthday.

OR *Sally* | had a microcomputer | from her parents for her birthday.
            got a microcomputer | for her birthday from her parents.
            received a microcomputer

b) *The news* | was | so bad that Helen burst into tears.
                      so bad that it made Helen burst into tears.

c) *When* | did you last see Mary?
           did you see Mary last?

OR *When* | was it (that) you saw Mary last?
            was the last time (that) you saw Mary?   (2 marks)

d) *Unless* | he works harder, he'll lose his job. | (2 marks)

e) *India is* | the country | I'd like to visit most.
                             I would like to visit most.
                             I should like to visit most.

OR *India is* | the country | . . . to visit more than any other country.
                                          anywhere in the world.

f) *Alan wished* | he had | never asked Arthur to lend | *him £20.*
                            not asked

g) *Martha asked Peter when* | the first day of his holiday | was. |

OR | his holiday began.
                               started.   (2 marks)

h) *It took* | three and a half hours to fly to Moscow. | (2 marks)

              to get to Moscow | by air.
              to go to Moscow
              to reach Moscow

i) *There* | are more than a thousand employees | in the factory where I work.
                       over a thousand employees | that I work in.
                                                  | in which I work.

OR *There* | are . . . employees | in my factory.
                                  | our

j) *Belinda went to the party* | even though she felt depressed.
                                 | although she felt depressed.
                                 | though she felt depressed.
                                 | in spite of feeling depressed.
                                 | despite feeling depressed.   (2 marks)

Total: 22

Question 3   Give one mark for each correct answer.

a) got away with
b) get out of
c) get out/off
d) get back/get there/get home
e) get by

Total: 5

Question 4   Give one mark for each correct answer.

a) carelessly
b) straighten
c) plentiful
d) unreliable
e) conclusion

Total: 5

Question 5

Give one mark for each word or phrase between the vertical lines, or two marks where shown.
(Ignore the words printed in italics.)

a) *Thank you* | very much | for the | *letter* | inviting | *me*
                 | so much | for your | | in which you invite
                                                  | in which you invited
                                                  | in which you have invited

    | to speak | to | *your students* | on | *careers* | in | the | *airline industry.*
                                       | about

43

b) *I* | would be | delighted | to | *come* | and | answer
will be | | | | | | give answers to
should be
shall be

(all) the | *questions* | your | *students have.*
whatever | | the
any

c) *Generally I find (that) it* | is | *best* | to | *start* | by | showing

a video film | followed | by | *a discussion.*
video films
some video films

OR | and (then) follow (it) | with a discussion.

d) *Also, I have* | a | *wide selection* | of | *information leaflets which I*

shall | *bring* | and give (out) | to | *any students* | who
am going to | | to give (out)
will
would
can
could

are | *interested.*
may be
might be

OR | if | *any students* | are | *interested.*

e) *You (have) suggest(ed) (that) any day in* | the | *last week* | of | *March*

will be | *suitable.*
would be
is

f) | *I* | *am* | *afraid that I* | 'll be | | *at* | *a* | *conference* | *in* | *Lima then.* |

am going to be / have to be / will be / shall be

the

g) | *However, I* | can | *manage* | *to* | *come* | on | | *2nd or 10th April.* |

could

either / on either / either on

h) | *Please let* | *me* | *know which* | *of* | *these dates* |

is
will be
would be

convenient.

i) | *I look forward* | *to* | *hearing* | *from* | *you.* |

Divide total of 46 by 2 = 23

Question 6

This part of the paper is intended to test the candidate's ability to use information and present a relevant answer in continuous form, with coherence and the right emphasis.

Give an impression mark of 0 to 7 for each paragraph, taking into account the candidate's ability to select relevant information, and link it in an appropriate and meaningful way, using concise and accurate sentences.

Total: 14

Paper 4: Listening Comprehension (about 30 minutes)

Part one: Decorating

			Score
1	wallpaper	√	½
2	green paint		½
3	white paint	√	½
4	paint brushes	√	½
5	brush for paste		½
6	bucket	√	½
7	newspapers		½
8	scissors		½
9	paste	√	½

Total: 4½ marks

Part two: Tariq learns to swim

		Score
10	C	1
11	D	1
12	B	1
13	B	1

Total: 4 marks

Part three: Conference timetable

		Score
14	10.30 am	½
15	Common Room	1
16	Teachers' Room	1
17	Principal's Office	1
18	Main Hall	1
19	Tour	1
20	2 pm	½
21	Film Show	1
22	4 pm	½
23	Finish	1

Total: 8½ marks

Part four: Advertisement for new homes

		Score
24 F		½
25 T		½
26 F		½
27 T		½
28 T		½
29 F		½

Total: 3 marks

Total marks: 20

Transcript

Cambridge First Certificate in English.

Test Number 3

You will be given a question paper and separate answer sheet for First Certificate Test 3. There are four parts to the test and each part will be heard twice. During the test, there will be pauses before each part to allow you to look through the questions, and other pauses to let you think about your answers. At the end of every pause you will hear this sound.

tone

You should write your answers on the question paper. You will have five minutes at the end to transfer your answers to the separate answer sheet.

The tape will now be stopped while question papers are given out. You must ask any questions now, as you will not be allowed to speak during the test.

pause

Part one

You will hear a conversation between two people about decorating a room. For questions 1 to 9, tick the boxes to show which items they need to get from the shop.

pause

tone

DECORATING

Woman: Yes, I think that's definitely the best pattern. It certainly goes best with the curtains. Let's go down to Slades and get all the things that we need for the decorating now.

Man: Well, wallpaper's the first thing, um, how many rolls do you think we need?

Woman: Oh I don't know, it's going to work out at about six or seven I think.

Man: Best to be on the safe side, let's get seven. Um, want some paste as well don't we. Um, yeah, write that one down then. So that's seven rolls of paper and um some paste, now what about the ceiling, are we going to paper that?

Woman: Oh no, I shouldn't think so, we can just paint it.

Man:	What colour do you think, um, I'd have thought green, wouldn't you, go with the wallpaper.
Woman:	Oh, I think white for ceilings, I mean I think all the ceilings white would be better.
Man:	Uh-huh. Well how much do you think we'll need for that?
Woman:	Oh, just one large tin should be enough.
Man:	Right, um. . . .
Woman:	Have we got any paint brushes?
Man:	I think we've got one or two old ones, but uh, we could do with some new ones, yes, let's get one or two new paint brushes then.
Woman:	What about a brush for the wallpaper paste?
Man:	Well, one of the old ones would do for that, wouldn't it . . .
Woman:	Oh yes that'll be all right fine . . .
Man:	Anything else we need?
Woman:	Um, could do with a bucket to make the paste in.
Man:	That's a good idea. Right. Um, what about something to cut the paper up with? We've got your old, we've got your scissors, haven't we?
Woman:	What, my dressmaking scissors, yes I suppose we could use them.
Man:	Yes okay, um, and something to cover the floor so we don't get paste all over the carpet. There's some old newspapers in the cupboard, aren't there?
Woman:	Yes, yeah, that's fine . . .
Man:	Okay?

pause

tone
Now you will hear the piece again. [The piece is repeated.]

pause

That is the end of the first part of the test.

pause

Part two
You will hear a radio programme in which an author, Hassina Khan, talks about a book she has written. For each of the questions 10 to 13, tick one of the boxes A, B, C or D to show the correct answer.

pause

tone

TARIQ LEARNS TO SWIM

Presenter:	"Tariq learns to swim" it's called. It's a picture-book for children about Tariq, who's from an Asian country, but lives with his parents and goes to school in England, his sister Yasmin, and certain problems that he has. There's a picture of him in a street full of comfortable-looking parents and children, mostly white. "He felt lonely and left out," says the text.
	Well, the book is written by Hassina Khan, who's English by birth, but married to a businessman from Pakistan. They live in London with their three children who have been brought up in the Muslim

faith. Hassina Khan told Kathleen Cheeseman how she came to write the book.

Hassina Khan: Well, it began when my eldest daughter, Shanah, who is now eight, began school, and I was concerned that her class fellows may notice some differences in her and wouldn't understand, for instance, why she had to have days off to go to the Mosque, or why she sometimes wore different clothes, and this sort of thing. And so I volunteered to explain to all the children at the school about the different customs, traditions, clothes, food, etc. And – um – the talks went down extremely well. I wore traditional costume, and took titbits in for the children to eat, and it was quite a treat for them. And, because of the success of this, I thought I would write a few stories, and uh – it just snowballed from there.

Kathleen Cheeseman: Well in this book, Tariq, your young hero, and his family – they're obviously Asians living in Britain, and you can tell that from the pictures. But there's no direct mention of it in the text. So how important do you want that to be for the reader?

Hassina Khan: I just want it to reflect the fact that within the British community, there are all shades of people and – uh – the Tariq book has a central character who is Asian, and this is fairly normal.

Kathleen Cheeseman: Well, young Tariq, who is about seven or eight, I suppose, has this problem that he doesn't like playing football. All the other boys play football. And this seems to be the most serious matter in *his* life.

Hassina Khan: Yes, I think all children have many of these sorts of crises in their lives. And – um – they overcome them in different ways. It's just a simple exercise in confidence-building. It's just a very gentle book.

Kathleen Cheeseman: Well Tariq's father comes up with the solution that he should learn to swim, and that's his way of impressing the other children – so – er – perhaps that might suggest similar solutions to other young people . . .

Hassina Khan: Yes, if you can't do one thing, you might be good at another. Quite.

pause

tone

Now you will hear the piece again. [The piece is repeated.]

pause

That is the end of the second part of the test.

pause

Part three
You will hear someone giving details about a timetable to a group of people at a conference. For questions 14 to 23 fill in the missing information on the revised timetable in the spaces provided.

pause

tone

CONFERENCE TIMETABLE

. . . Well, ladies and gentlemen, um, I'm sure, er, you're all anxious to get on with your discussions and, um, er, I, er think now more or less everybody is here, so, er, if, um, if you'd just like to er, listen for a moment I need to run through the programme because, um, there have been one or two alterations, as, as we're running a bit late, um because of people being held up by the bad weather, um, I er, um, now first of all, um we're not going to start off the day with a tour for the new members, um, because this will enable us to catch up again with the time we've lost. Now if any members are particularly anxious to see round the buildings, if they would like to go round in the lunch hour, um, they could eat up their lunch a little bit quickly and then um, we could show them round before the afternoon session begins.

Um, now, it's now um, ten-fifteen, and we'd very much like to get going by ten-thirty um, which will give you two hours, er, full hours, to get back um, for the full meeting with um, some sort of conclusions, um, perhaps. So, if I could just tell you your rooms again, um, Group A, I think you probably all know who you are, don't you, which group you're in – now Group A, you're in the Common Room, and Group B are in the Teachers' Room, um, but Group C, er, you are not in the Library as, er, as stated in the letter you had last week, um, Group C you are in fact going to be in the Principal's Office, because the Library heating isn't working very well, and with this awful weather we're having, it's really very cold indeed in there, so, um, we're most grateful to the Principal for, um, allowing us to use his office, um, for Group C, OK?

Um, now, um, the lunch will be from um, one to two as usual, um, and in that hour, if anyone would like to fit in a tour, please could you let me know now, before you leave the room. Um, so that's lunch, and that'll be back here in the Main Hall.

At two o'clock, please be punctual, if you, you know, for the um, film show. Um, we'll see the film and then um, there'll be an opportunity for informal discussion with colleagues, um, over a cup of tea before the formal questioning session at four o'clock, or about four o'clock, er, when you will be able to raise points with Professor Dunn and his team about their ideas. Um, and then we hope that we'll all be able to get off home by five o'clock. Er, which in view of this rather nasty weather, I think would be a good thing, not to be delayed. Right, ladies and gentlemen, thank you very much. Does anyone have any questions?

pause

tone
Now you will hear the piece again. [The piece is repeated.]

pause

That is the end of the third part of the test.

pause

Part four
You will hear an advertisement for new houses. For each of the questions 24 to 29 tick one box to show whether the statements are true or false.

pause

tone

ADVERTISEMENT FOR NEW HOMES

. . . Charter Homes here with the fantastic news that you could part-exchange your old house for one of our beautiful new three- and four-bedroomed black and white Tudor-style houses here at Squiredale, Norton Farm.

You can reserve now at specially low prices whilst we're putting the finishing touches to our new show homes.

We can arrange your mortgage, subject to status, as well as giving you free redundancy protection and with our generous part-exchange plan to help you, we could make your move even easier than you think. Come along and see us at Squiredale, College Lane, Norton Farm, or call us on Norton 310.

pause

tone
Now you will hear the piece again. [The piece is repeated.]

pause

That is the end of the fourth part of the test.

There will now be a five-minute pause to allow you to check your work and transfer your answers to the separate answer sheet. The question papers and answer sheets will then be collected by your supervisor.

pause

tone
That is the end of the test.

Paper 5: Interview (about 15 minutes)

THE MEDIA

The following sample package of oral examiner's material enables a complete interview to be practised and students' speaking skills to be assessed according to the marking scales given on pages 10–12. The photographs, passages and activities for Practice Test 3 can be found at the back of the Student's Book.

Photographs   (usually about 5 minutes)

Refer students to one or more of the photographs on pages 107–108 of the Student's Book.

18

19

20

Allow a suitable short interval for study, then open discussion along the lines suggested. Describe/compare the people; the setting; the activities.

The conversation should then lead on to an informal discussion of one or more of the following subjects:

– people's reasons for reading newspapers/listening to the radio/watching TV
– ways of finding out about the news
– what it would be like to be without radios/TVs/newspapers

Questions such as the following may help to lead the conversation in the right direction, although students should be encouraged to sustain their part in the conversation beyond simple question-and-answer.

Do you prefer to listen to the radio or watch television? Why?
What is the best way of finding out about the news?
Do you think life would be very different without newspapers/radio/television? How?
Are some people in danger of watching too much television?

Passages (usually about 2 minutes)

Refer students to one or more of the passages on page 108 of the Student's Book. Invite the students to try and link the themes of the passages to the photographs. For further discussion you may ask the students to comment on the passages, saying what sort of passages they are. Students should *not* be asked to read a whole passage aloud but may quote from it where this arises naturally during the course of the conversation.

21 I wish she would turn the radio down. All we hear from morning till night is music and news bulletins. The sound travels right through the walls in this place and we never have a minute's peace.

22 Excuse me! Do you think I could borrow your newspaper if you've finished with it? I didn't have time to buy one at the station this morning. I hope you don't mind me asking.

23 I don't know why you watch that rubbish on the TV. I can't stand it myself. There must be something more interesting than that on surely! And if there isn't, just switch it off and do something useful.

Tasks (usually about 5 minutes)

Choose one of the following tasks from Interview Exercises 24 and 25.

Discussion activity

Refer students to the cartoon printed below and on page 109 of the Student's Book. Invite reaction to it and then initiate a discussion about television and radio using the questions below as prompts.

24

- Should parents control what their children watch on television, listen to on the radio, read (books, magazines etc.)?
- Is it possible to listen to the radio and concentrate on other things at the same time e.g. drive a car safely, work effectively etc.?
- Should there be any censorship of radio/television programmes broadcast before 9.00 p.m.?
- Is television a good thing?

Activity

Refer students to the timetable of television programmes printed below and on page 109 of the Student's Book.

Invite the students to imagine that they are free to watch something between 8.00 p.m. and 10.00 p.m. Ask them to decide which programme to watch and give reasons for their choice. It is possible to adapt this activity as a role play, assigning the following roles to students:

Role A – you love sport
Role B – you like music and comedy
Role C – you like serious, informative programmes

25

Channel 1		Channel 2		Channel 3		Channel 4
.0pm	**Bread** More comedy with the hilarious family from Liverpool	8.00pm	**Wildlife in Tasmania** Nature documentary	8.00pm	**Football** Albania v. England Live coverage of the whole of this World Cup qualifying match from Tirana	8.00pm **Happy Days** Classic American comedy series
.0pm	**By Bike Across China** Travel documentary	9.00pm	**News**			8.30pm **The Sound of Music** A romantic musical film based on a real life story in wartime Austria
		9.30pm	**News EXTRA** Discussion of current issues	10.00pm	**News**	
.0pm	**World War II** Part 10. Continuing this important history series	10.00pm	**Sportsnight**			10.00pm **News**
.0pm	**News**					

Practice Test 4

Paper 1: Reading Comprehension (1 hour)

Section A   Give one mark for each correct answer.

1 C	6 A	11 B	16 A	21 A
2 A	7 D	12 C	17 B	22 C
3 A	8 C	13 B	18 A	23 B
4 A	9 D	14 D	19 B	24 A
5 C	10 D	15 A	20 D	25 C

Section B   Give two marks for each correct answer.

26 B	31 C	36 C
27 D	32 D	37 B
28 B	33 C	38 D
29 C	34 D	39 A
30 A	35 D	40 C

Total: 55

Paper 2: Composition (1 ½ hours)

See pages 3–7 for mark scheme and sample compositions.

Paper 3: Use of English (2 hours)

A complete mark scheme is given for each question. The 'raw' total of 80 for this paper would be adjusted to a mark out of 40 in the exam itself. Candidates passing the examination as a whole would be expected to score about 60% of the total marks.

Question 1   Give one mark for each correct answer.

1 her/Laura's
2 an
3 and
4 had/originally/initially/first/Ashley
5 at/from
6 but
7 made
8 By
9 into
10 far
11 of/with
12 is/was
13 in/with
14 it
15 should/would
16 a/another
17 whose
18 fell/slipped/tumbled
19 while/whilst/when
20 later/afterwards/after

Total: 20

Question 2

Give one mark for each word or phrase between the vertical lines, or two marks where shown.
(Ignore the words printed in italics.)

a) *Mr Hill's students* | are (being) taught (how) to understand different (English) accents. |
are learning (how)   to hear
             to distinguish   (2 marks)

b) *The film* | was so boring   (that) | we left before the end. |
was such a boring one   did not stay until the end.
bored us so much   till the end. |

c) *It's four years* | since Robert and Catherine | got married. |
             they   were married. |

d) *If Elizabeth* | had not started smoking (cigarettes) |
hadn't begun

  she would not have got   a (bad) cough. |
      wouldn't have had
              developed

e) *Anna asked* her mother | if | she could have   a new bicycle. |
             whether   give her
                      get her
                      buy her

f) *It's not* | my fault if   the tin-opener is broken. |
          that   has (been) broken. | (2 marks)

g) *In spite* | of his (bad) cold | William (still) went to work. |
      a (bad) cold   he
      his suffering from a (bad) cold |

h) *Mike doesn't* | play squash as well as Barbara (does). |
                 so   (2 marks)

i) *Who does* | this suitcase belong to? |
         case   (2 marks)

j) *It is a* | two-hour train journey from London to Bristol. |
     2-hour   (2 marks)

Total: 20

Question 3   Give one mark for each correct answer.

a) only
b) single/one-way
c) alone
d) singular
e) unique

Total: 5

Question 4   Give one mark for each correct answer.

a) sweeter
b) tough/gristly/stringy/leathery
c) fresh
d) taste
e) sour/curdled/off

Total: 5

Question 5

Give 2 marks for each item – any correct and appropriate answer is acceptable. Deduct one mark for any error however slight, or for repetition. Deduct two marks for major errors. For example,

2 I couldn't afford it = 2
   I haven't some money = (1 error)
   I haven't got time = 0 (inappropriate)

6 . . . I find out more about these hostels? = 2
   . . . I get a leaflet? = 1 (repetition)

Other 2-mark answers:

1 *I wish I* had gone with you.
3 *Aren't* Youth Hostels meant to be for students?
4 *Can* you have meals there?
5 *What* was the food like?

Total: 12

Question 6

Award 0–6 marks for each paragraph.
   The task is one of giving opinions and reasons in the light of the given data and expressing relevant points with clarity, conciseness and a reasonable degree of fluency.
   Fluent, mature answers may be awarded the maximum 6 marks, even if they contain one or two minor errors. Answers which have major grammatical errors or show a lack of coherence or syntactical control should be awarded no more than 2.

Total: 18

Paper 4: Listening Comprehension (about 30 minutes)

Part one: Road accident

	True	False	Score
1		✓	½
2		✓	½
3	✓		½
4		✓	½
5	✓		½
6	✓		½
7		✓	½
8	✓		½
9		✓	½
10		✓	½

Total: 5 marks

Part two: Birthday present

(Allow use of capitals but no spelling mistakes in this copying exercise.)

		Score
11	record(s)	1
12	book(s)	1
13	perfume	1
14	food	1
15	glasses	1

Total: 5 marks

Part three: Gas cooker

		Score
16	√	½
17	√	½
18	√	½
19		½
20	√	½
21	√	½
22	√	½
23	√	½
24		½
25		½

Total: 5 marks

Part four: Recipeline

		Score
26	B	1
27	C	1
28	Pancakes/Pan Cakes (must be spelt correctly)	½
29	flour	1
30	milk (must be spelt correctly)	½
31	(the) eggs/egs	1

Total: 5 marks

Total marks: 20

Transcript

Cambridge First Certificate in English.
Test Number 4
You will be given a question paper and separate answer sheet for First Certificate Test 4. There are four parts to the test and each part will be heard twice. During the test, there will be pauses before each part to allow you to look through the questions, and other pauses to let you think about your answers. At the end of every pause you will hear this sound.

tone

You should write your answers on the question paper. You will have five minutes at the end to transfer your answers to the separate answer sheet.
   The tape will now be stopped while question papers are given out. You must ask any questions now, as you will not be allowed to speak during the test.

pause

Part one
You will hear a court case about a road accident. For each of the questions 1 to 10, tick one box to show whether each statement is true or false.

pause

tone

ROAD ACCIDENT

Clerk of Court:	Call Martha Dobbs. Right. Take the book in your right hand and repeat after me: I swear *(she repeats phrase by phrase)* that the evidence I shall give shall be the truth, the whole truth, and nothing but the truth. Thank you.
Counsel:	You are Martha Dobbs?
Martha Dobbs:	Yes, that's right.
Counsel:	And you live at 42 West Mansions, South Everly?
Martha Dobbs:	Yes, I do.
Counsel:	Thank you. Will you please tell the court where you were on the afternoon of Tuesday 22nd December, at about 3 o'clock?
Martha Dobbs:	Yes. I was in town doing some shopping – you know one or two last-minute things I had to get done before the Christmas holiday. And um I was walking along the High Street near where it joins West Road – you know, where the pedestrian crossing is . . .
Counsel:	Yes . . .
Martha Dobbs:	and . . . when suddenly I noticed a motor-cycle coming along the road at great speed . . .
Counsel:	Have you any idea how fast it was going?
Martha Dobbs:	Oh, well, no, I should say at least about 45 miles an hour . . .
Counsel:	In a built-up area?
Martha Dobbs:	Of course.
Counsel:	3 o'clock on a December afternoon. Was it light or dark at the time?
Martha Dobbs:	Just getting dark. It were one of those dark, dismal days . . .
Counsel:	Was it raining at the time?
Martha Dobbs:	Yes, fairly heavily. But there was enough light to see very clearly what happened.

Counsel:	And what did happen?
Martha Dobbs:	Well, just at that moment a pedestrian started to cross the road at a zebra crossing.
Counsel:	Could you describe the pedestrian?
Martha Dobbs:	Yes. He was an elderly man wearing glasses and carrying a walking stick. He didn't seem to look right nor left before crossing, and he didn't seem to hear the motor-bike at all. Perhaps he was deaf . . . *(Silence in court!)*
Counsel:	And what happened then?
Martha Dobbs:	Well, there was this red car just approaching the crossing. And it pulled up dead, and the motor-cyclist tried to swerve to avoid hitting the car, but he didn't have time, as he was going too fast, and crashed right into it. He was thrown from the bike, and he landed right in the middle of the pedestrian crossing.
Counsel:	And the pedestrian?
Martha Dobbs:	Oh, he just managed to get across.
Counsel:	Now, do you by any chance happen to remember the licence number of the motor-cycle?
Martha Dobbs:	Yes, it was an easy number to remember: DIY 220 U.
Counsel:	And the car?
Martha Dobbs:	No, no I didn't see that, I'm afraid, well, 'cause it was right beside me at the time of the accident.
Counsel:	Thank you very much, Mrs Dobbs.
Martha Dobbs:	Miss Dobbs. *(Silence in court!)*

pause

tone

Now you will hear the piece again. [The piece is repeated.]

pause

That is the end of the first part of the test.

pause

Part two

You will hear a conversation about birthday presents. Choose from the following list the items that best match the opinions expressed and write them in the spaces numbered 11 to 15.

pause

tone

BIRTHDAY PRESENT

Woman:	Isn't it your mother's birthday next week, it's on the seventeenth isn't it, that's that's Wednesday I think. . . .
Man:	Wednesday, Wednesday, yes, yes.
Woman:	We'd better get a present today so we get it in time to put it in the post.
Man:	Uh, yes what d'you think she'd like?
Woman:	Oh, I don't know, we have this problem every year. What about perfume?
Man:	Perfume? Um, yes, well she likes expensive perfume but uh we gave her some, didn't we give her some for Christmas?

Woman: Oh yes, we did. What about books?

Man: Um, well, she's a member of a book club so she's always likely, to have um any book you want to give her, I mean she's, . . . the house is full of books . . .

Woman: Yes, yes, that's true, yes. Um, I suppose we could think about a record . . .

Man: Yes, that's possible, but I don't know, I always feel giving her a record . . . she she never really plays them very much, I don't think she listens to music a great deal, um, let's keep that idea in reserve. Um, I tell you what she does like, um, nice glasses . . .

Woman: What, you mean wine glasses, *(yes)* brandy glasses, that sort of thing . . . um, good ones are very expensive, very dear, but I suppose if we could find some at a reasonable price that'd be, that'd be a good idea.

Man: Um, what do we call a reasonable price?

Woman: Oh, I think we've got to certainly spend ten pounds, aren't we, something like that, or even a bit more, she's always very generous to all of us.

Man: Um yes, I think that's a possibility actually, good idea. Anything else, um, something in the food line perhaps?

Woman: Oh no, she's supposed to be on a diet, so I don't think that's a very good idea!

pause

tone

Now you will hear the piece again. [The piece is repeated.]

pause

That is the end of the second part of the test.

pause

Part three

You will hear a woman talking about a new kind of gas cooker. For questions 16 to 25, tick the boxes to show which of the following features have been mentioned. If the feature is not mentioned, leave the box blank.

pause

tone

GAS COOKER

Good morning ladies and gentlemen. How nice to see such a lot of people in front of me.

Well, as you know I am here to demonstrate the new de Luxe Gas Cooker. You can see on first glance that it is a modern, smart and attractive cooker. And I can tell you, ladies and gentlemen, that the price is a realistic one – this cooker is great value for money! *(Yes, but what does it do?)*

Just let me show you some of its attractions: you can see that it is a compact cooker – it does not take up a lot of space – and some parts of it can even be conveniently folded away.

Let's start at the top . . . The essential plate rack, on which to keep your plates warm while cooking. And just below, here, is the grill which, as you can see, can be neatly folded away. To open the grill and fold it back again all you need to do is to press this lever here which is at the side of the grill on the right. Just that little lever on the right.

The main cooking area below the grill is the hotplate with its four high speed burners.

These burners can be adjusted to any cooking rate from a very fast boil right down to a gentle simmer. And at the front of the hotplate you can see the four round taps on the right hand side which you use to regulate the size of the flame of the burners. The remaining round tap on the left hand side is for the oven which you can see below the hotplate. Notice the glass plate on the oven door. You don't need to open the oven door while cooking – just look through the glass plate to see how your cooking is getting on. To see more clearly there is a light inside the oven. The button to work this is the square one over here, just above the oven tap to the left. Press the button and the light will come on.

To light the oven and the hotplate all you do is press the automatic lighter which is the square button here above the oven tap to the right. Very convenient, you see. And if you want to go out for the day, you can put the oven on automatic. There's nothing like coming home to the smell of a meal ready cooked, just waiting to be eaten. And to set the oven to automatic you will need to use the control clock which is the one here, just below the grill.

Finally, below the oven, at the bottom here, there's a fold-away drawer which you can use to store your roasting dishes and grill pan.

Now I think that's all I have to say – would anyone like to ask me some questions? *(Yes please has it got a guarantee?)* Oh yes indeed, there's certainly a guarantee, it's a three-year guarantee, Madam. . . .

pause

tone
Now you will hear the piece again. [The piece is repeated.]

pause

That is the end of the third part of the test.

pause

Part four
You will hear a recorded telephone announcement giving a recipe for stuffed pancakes. For each of the questions 26 and 27, tick one of the boxes A, B, C or D to show which is the correct answer. For questions 28 to 31, fill in the missing information in the spaces provided.

pause

tone

RECIPELINE

Hello – hope you've all got your pencils ready. You will need half a litre of pancake mixture, and for the filling, one onion, chopped, 25 grams of butter, 25 grams of flour, half a litre of milk, 50 grams of cheese, grated, half a bunch of watercress, chopped, four hard-boiled eggs, roughly chopped and seasoning.

Now to make: make eight pancakes and keep warm. Fry onions in butter, stir in flour and cook for a further two minutes. Remove from heat, add milk, and bring to the boil. Cook for two minutes. Add the cheese and watercress to the sauce with the eggs. Season and divide between the pancakes. Roll them up and reheat. That's all for now, and I'll be back tomorrow with another recipe.

pause

tone
Now you will hear the piece again. [The piece is repeated.]

pause

That is the end of the fourth part of the test.

There will now be a five-minute pause to allow you to check your work and transfer your answers to the separate answer sheet. The question papers and answer sheets will then be collected by your supervisor.

pause

tone
That is the end of the test.

Paper 5: Interview (about 15 minutes)

SPORT

The following sample package of oral examiner's material enables a complete interview to be practised and students' speaking skills to be assessed according to the marking scales given on pages 10–12. The photographs, passages and activities for Practice Test 4 can be found at the back of the Student's Book.

Photographs   (usually about 5 minutes)

Refer the students to one or more of the photographs on pages 110–111 of the Student's Book.

26

27

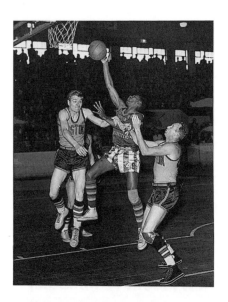

28

Allow a suitable short interval for study, then open discussion along the lines suggested.
a) Describe/compare the activity; the people; the setting.
b) The conversation should then lead on to an informal discussion of one or more of the following subjects:

  – the student's own sporting interests
  – most popular sport in the student's country
  – watching sport on television

If two or three students are being interviewed together, encourage individuals to initiate a discussion on one topic, and invite the other students to comment.

Questions such as the following may help to lead the conversation in the right direction, although students should be encouraged to sustain their part in the conversation beyond simple question-and-answer.

– What sports are you interested in?
– What are the most popular sports in your country?
– What is different about going to a sporting event and watching it on television?
– Do you think it's necessary to practise a sport in order to keep fit?

Passages   (usually about 2 minutes)

Refer students to one or more of the passages: Interview Exercises 29, 30 and 31 at the back of the Student's Book. Ask the students to comment on the passages, saying where they think the extracts may have been taken from. Invite the students to try and link the themes of the passages to the photographs. Students should *not* be asked to read a whole passage aloud but may quote from it where this arises naturally during the course of the conversation.

29   "What an experience! We never thought we'd see sportsmen like that in real life – something to tell everyone at home about. They must have to train 24 hours a day!"

30   Manchester United manager Alex Ferguson last night tipped Norwich to claim the League title. He took his team home from East Anglia after a 2–1 defeat saying "Norwich are good enough to go all the way."

31   Past Glories is now completely fit again after recovering from a leg injury sustained last summer. He has had several good gallops recently, but I am more impressed by the form of Fu's Lady. She should win on Saturday, with Silver Ace a close second.

Tasks   (usually about 5 minutes)

Choose one or both of the following activities:

Refer students to the list of people in Interview Exercise 32 at the back of the Student's Book. Invite candidates to discuss the needs of and to make suggestions as to the most suitable sports or physical activities for some or all of the following people:

32
a) a retired person, reasonably fit, has a lot of free time
b) a housewife, would like to take up an activity while her young children are at nursery school
c) a middle-aged businessman, overweight and with very little free time, wants to get fit
d) a student, wants to do something energetic and to meet people – something competitive perhaps

Refer students to the cartoon in Interview Exercise 33 at the back of the Student's Book and invite reaction to it. Encourage discussion along the following lines:

- reasons for doing daily exercises
- current popularity of keep-fit and physical training
- exercising versus sport as a means of health
- possible dangers of over-exertion of any kind

33

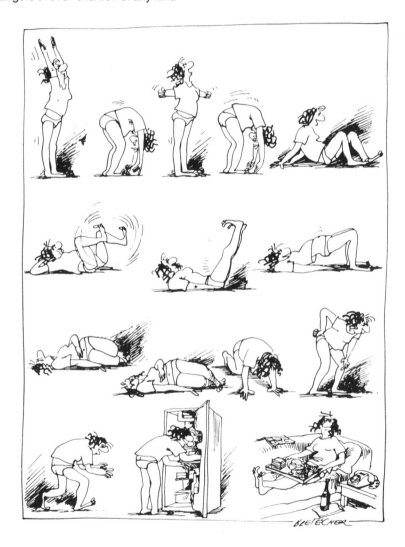

Practice Test 5

Paper 1: Reading Comprehension (1 hour)

Section A   Give one mark for each correct answer.

1 A	6 C	11 D	16 C	21 D
2 C	7 B	12 A	17 B	22 A
3 B	8 C	13 B	18 D	23 B
4 B	9 A	14 B	19 B	24 A
5 B	10 B	15 B	20 D	25 D

Section B   Give two marks for each correct answer.

26 C	31 D	36 D
27 A	32 C	37 B
28 B	33 B	38 B
29 D	34 A	39 C
30 A	35 C	40 C

Total: 55

Paper 2: Composition (1 ½ hours)

See pages 3–7 for mark scheme and sample compositions.

Paper 3: Use of English (2 hours)

A complete mark scheme is given for each question. The 'raw' total of 90 for this paper would be adjusted to a mark out of 40 in the exam itself. Candidates passing the examination as a whole would be expected to score about 60% of the total marks.

Question 1   Give one mark for each correct answer.

1 was	11 by
2 for	12 still
3 working	13 has
4 who	14 where
5 and	15 One/Another
6 started/begun/commenced	16 was
7 is/forms	17 answers/solutions
8 on	18 most
9 which	19 died
10 of	20 named

Total: 20

Question 2

Give one mark for each word or phrase between the vertical lines, or two marks where shown. (Ignore the words printed in italics.)

a) *Was* | the garage built | at the same time as the house?   (2 marks)

b) *Nobody who* | was at the meeting | will say anything to the press. |

c) *We were* | not able   to have   our picnic | because of   (the) (heavy) rain. |
             unable   owing to
             prevented from having   due to
             stopped   on account of
                                      as a consequence of

d) *If* | Joan doesn't find a good job before September | she will stay on at school. |
     she   manage to find   Joan

e) *I'd rather* | not | go out tonight. |

f) *It wasn't* | until she   was eight | that Shirley began to read. |
          Shirley   she   began reading.
                                    started to read.
                                    started reading.

g) *The last* | time (that) Lucy wore that dress | was | *at Barbara's wedding.*
                                               | *when Barbara got married.*

h) *Why* | don't we | *go abroad for our holiday this year* | ? |

i) *He speaks* | so | slowly (that) | *his students get very bored.*

j) *By the age of twenty* | Mackenzie had written | four best-sellers. |
                            he   (2 marks)

Total: 20

Question 3 Give one mark for each correct answer.

a) dictionary
b) programme/program
c) brochures
d) timetable/time-table
e) directory/book/(tele)phone book

Total: 5

Question 4 Give one mark for each correct answer.

a) making
b) held
c) turned/showed
d) stand up to
e) took/has taken/is taking

Total: 5

Question 5

Give **half** a mark for each phrase or word between the vertical lines. (Ignore the words printed in italics.)

a) *I* | am writing | in | *reply* | to | *your advertisement* | in yesterday's |

   'Evening Guardian'.

b) | In it you say (that) | you are looking | for | a | *secretary*
   | said (that) | were looking |

   | with good | *typing skills who* | must be | *fluent* | in French | and English. |
   | | | is |

c) *I* | have just completed | the | *two-year bilingual secretarial course*
   | | a |

   | at | *my local college.*

d) *At* | the | *end* | of | the | *course I* | passed all | my | *exams*
   | | | | my | | | the |

   | with good | *marks.*

e) *Before* | I started it | I spent / I'd spent / I had spent | a / one | *year* | in France

| living with | a | *French family.*

f) *While* | I was there | I learned / I learnt | *(how)* | to speak French | *fluently.*

g) | I will be / I shall / I would / I should / I'll / I'd | *grateful* | if | you'd send me / you could / you would |

(some) more information about | the / this | *job* | with / and | the / an | *application form.*

h) *I look forward* | to | *hearing* | from | *you.*

Total: 19

Question 6

Award 0–7 marks for each paragraph.

The task is one of giving opinions and reasons in the light of the given data and expressing relevant points with clarity, conciseness and a reasonable degree of fluency.

Fluent, reasoned answers may be awarded the maximum 7 marks, even if they contain one or two minor errors. Answers which have major grammatical errors or show a lack of coherence or syntactical control should be awarded no more than 2.

Total: 21

Paper 4: Listening Comprehension (about 30 minutes)

Part one: Two sisters

		Score
1	D	1
2	C	1
3	B	1
4	C	1

Total: 4 marks

Part two: Melanie's house III

		Score
5	✓	½
6	✓	½
7	✓	½
8	–	½
9	✓	½
10	–	½
11	–	½
12	–	½
13	✓	½
14	–	½

Total: 5 marks

Part three: Dingles

		Score
15	£27.50	1
16	£18.99	½
17	£12.99	½
18	£14.99	½
19	£8.99	½
20	£10.00	½
21	£2.99	1
22	£1.99	½
23	8 (pm)	½
24	Thursday	1

Total: 6½ marks

Total marks: 15½

Transcript

Cambridge First Certificate in English.
Test Number 5
You will be given a question paper and separate answer sheet for First Certificate Test 5. There are three parts to the test and each part will be heard twice. During the test, there will be pauses before each part to allow you to look through the questions, and other pauses to let you think about your answers. At the end of every pause you will hear this sound.

tone

You should write your answers on the question paper. You will have five minutes at the end to transfer your answers to the separate answer sheet.

    The tape will now be stopped while question papers are given out. You must ask any questions now, as you will not be allowed to speak during the test.

pause

Part one
You will hear two sisters discussing their father's illness. For questions 1 to 4 tick one of the boxes A, B, C or D to show the correct answer.

pause

tone

TWO SISTERS

Sister A: I'm absolutely exhausted, we had to get up four times again last night. Dad will keep trying to get out of bed at night and I'm so frightened of him falling, he's so weak.

Sister B: Well you can't go on like this, you'll make yourself ill. It would be different if you weren't working, but Dad needs constant attention now. He should really be in a hospital. He doesn't understand what's going on most of the time and in a hospital . . .

Sister A: There's no question of him going to a hospital – it would kill him. He's happy here and he knows where he is. He would be absolutely lost in a strange place.

Sister B: Well I could have him at weekends and . . .

Sister A: How could he get up your stairs? Can you see us trying to get him up those stairs?

Sister B: But that's the whole point – because of the stairs he can't even go out any more. In a hospital they would have him in a wheelchair and take him outside in the nice weather. He might make some friends . . .

Sister A: How could he make friends – he doesn't recognise people or understand what they're saying properly.

Sister B: Precisely. In that case he wouldn't realise he was in hospital and at least he'd be getting proper medical attention.

Sister A: Oh no, he'd be miserable. He enjoys it when we watch the television together in the evening and I couldn't bear to think of him sitting in some hospital ward all alone. You don't understand, you don't spend as much time with him as I do. I understand what he feels. I'm not having him taken off to some hospital. I can look after him better than anybody else. You don't feel these things as I do. I know what's best for him. I want to do everything I can for him.

Sister B: It's no good getting upset. I know it's a difficult decision to make but I'm thinking of you too. You say yourself you can't go on like this for much longer and Dad's only going to get weaker and weaker. You won't be able to cope. Both you and Robert have problems with your backs, you won't be able to lift him and you know the effect it's having on Robert, looking after him all day. He's only just retired, he should be enjoying his retirement, instead of that he can't even go out. We have to think of him too.

Sister A: But I am thinking of him. It's a terrible problem. I only wish there was a solution but I couldn't bear to come home in the evening and not see Dad sitting there in his armchair. It's so important for me to know . . .

pause

tone
Now you will hear the piece again. [The piece is repeated.]

pause

That is the end of the first part of the test.

pause

Part two
You will hear a woman talking about things which she wants for her new kitchen. For questions 5 to 14, tick the boxes next to the items of equipment which she wants. Leave the other boxes blank.

pause

tone

MELANIE'S HOUSE III

So my next large programme is to think exactly what I want to do with the kitchen, so that I get it in a state that I would like it, and I am rather fussy about my kitchen, um, I work very hard at work and when I come home one of my great pleasures is to unwind by cooking – which is something completely different to thinking about words during the day. And I read cookery books for fun. I find they're very good things to go to sleep over because recipes aren't very long. You can just read a couple of recipes and the book falls out of my hand as I go to sleep, and so I adapt recipes or I use them as a starting point and then invent something new. It never really is new because somebody's always done almost the same thing somewhere before, but it feels as if it's new – and it's something that gives me great pleasure. And so I know that I want a sink and a draining board, and I'd probably like either a second sink bowl, or a half-sink. I've seen some rather nice sinks which are one-and-a-half bowls, and I want a little freezer. And a rather larger fridge because I love making ice-cream, and you really can't make ice-cream seriously unless you have a freezer that is big enough to store it in, and to make a few mistakes, and to have the door open every now and again to take things out and put things in – and still keep it cold enough to keep the ice-cream frozen when it's made.

And I like a gas hob, because I like the control of cooking with gas. But I'm not crazy about a gas oven, so I think I'm going to try and have a combination of a gas hob for saucepans and frying pans, and an oven for casseroles. And in fact I've got a very small free-standing oven, it's about the size of a micro-wave oven and it runs off a normal plug –

just like a light or a lamp, and it's got a glass front, so it's a little bit like a stainless steel cupboard with a glass front which you plug in, and because it's small it heats up very rapidly. Er, also because it's small you couldn't cook, well, a three-course dinner with three hot courses, but it would take a large turkey or a couple of big birthday cakes, or something like that all at once. And I also like it because it's got a glass front, so if I'm making a soufflé I can watch the soufflé rise and I can whip it out at exactly the right moment, or I can watch my cake browning and make sure that it's not burning. But because it's a little free-standing oven it'll need to stand on top of something – so I'll lose a little bit of my work surface in the kitchen for the little oven.

And I don't like very much, I don't very much like having cupboards on the shelves, I prefer, sorry having cupboards on the walls – I prefer to have open shelves because I like seeing where my jars of pasta and rice and biscuits and things are. And I like collecting pretty jars, that's also quite good discipline – you don't lose things in the backs of cupboards, things that you've forgotten about, if they're all on open shelves you can always see what you've got and you can make sure that things aren't going mouldy in forgotten corners, so I shall probably have shelves on the walls.

pause

tone
Now you will hear the piece again. [The piece is repeated.]

pause

That is the end of the second part of the test.

pause

Part three
You will hear some announcements being made in a department store. For questions 15 to 24 fill in the missing information in the picture of the shop window below.

pause

tone

DINGLES

Ladies and Gentlemen, welcome to the House of Fraser sale. In our Men's Department, we have Coconut Club knitwear at less than half price. We have Wolsey round-necked sweaters in 48% acrylic, 45% cotton and 7% linen. Originally £27.50, they're now just £18.99. We have House of Fraser exclusive men's trousers in 75% polyester and 25% cotton – originally £18.99, they've been reduced to £12.99. We have shirts by Hardy Amies, in assorted sizes and colours – originally £14.99, they're now just £8.99. Our Menswear Department is on the ground floor.

Ladies and Gentlemen, for anyone spending £10 or over we're offering up to 4 hours free car parking at the Berkeley Place Car Park. Simply ask any assistant for details.

Ladies and Gentlemen, in our Children's Wear Department, there's one third off tee-shirt and shorts sets, in assorted colours and sizes, for the ages six to twenty-four months. Originally £2.99, they've been reduced to £1.99. There's one third off anoraks, in assorted colours, for the sizes 12–18 months. Originally £10.99, they're now just £6.99. Our Children's Department is on the first floor.

Ladies and Gentlemen, we'd like to remind you that this store is open till 8 o'clock every Thursday evening.

Ladies and Gentlemen, welcome to the House of Fraser sale. In our Furniture Department we have £20 off Millbrook quality furniture – hand-crafted, with hand-made frames.

pause

tone
Now you will hear the piece again. [The piece is repeated.]

pause

That is the end of the third part of the test.

There will now be a five-minute pause to allow you to check your work and transfer your answers to the separate answer sheet. The question papers and answer sheets will then be collected by your supervisor.

pause

tone
That is the end of the test.

Paper 5: Interview (about 15 minutes)

COMMUNITY SPIRIT

The following sample package of oral examiner's material enables a complete interview to be practised and students' speaking skills to be assessed according to the marking scales given on pages 10–12. The photographs, passages and activities for Practice Test 5 can be found at the back of the Student's Book.

Photographs   (usually about 5 minutes)

Refer the students to one or more of the photographs on pages 112–113 of the Student's Book.

34

35

36

Allow a suitable short interval for study, then open discussion along the lines suggested. Describe/compare the people; the occasion; the activity.

The conversation should then lead on to an informal discussion of one or more of the following subjects:

- the importance of being part of a group
- the pleasures of young children
- the problems of old age

Questions such as the following may help to lead the conversation in the right direction, although students should be encouraged to sustain their part in the conversation beyond simple question-and-answer.

Do you enjoy being part of a group?
What are the differences between singing, making music or dancing, on your own and in a group?
What kinds of things do young children enjoy doing together?
Why is it a good thing for old people to get together?
What problems are faced by old people living on their own?

Passages (usually about 2 minutes)

Refer students to one or more of the passages: Interview Exercises 37, 38 and 39 on page 113 of the Student's Book. Invite the students to try and link the themes of the passages to the photographs. For further discussion you may ask the students to comment on the passages, saying what sort of passages they are. Students should *not* be asked to read a whole passage aloud but may quote from it where this arises naturally during the course of the conversation.

37   Let The People Sing – at school, at church, in the street, in the home. Wherever people are, however bad things are, singing together makes life better, brings us all closer.

38   Spring 1989 Programme
We are a small but friendly group simply trying to enjoy life and help others to do the same. We have been in existence since 1932 and are always willing to welcome new members, no matter what age or nationality. So why not come along to one of our regular events this week or phone one of our Committee Members TODAY!

39   We love the tea room at the centre. It's somewhere you can go and have a chat and a laugh. Stops you feeling lonely, I can tell you!

Tasks (usually about 5 minutes)

Choose one of the following tasks from Interview Exercises 40 and 41.

Discussion

Refer students to the 'Free Introductions' advertisement for the *Opportunities Knock* Friendship Agency on page 114 of the Student's Book.

40

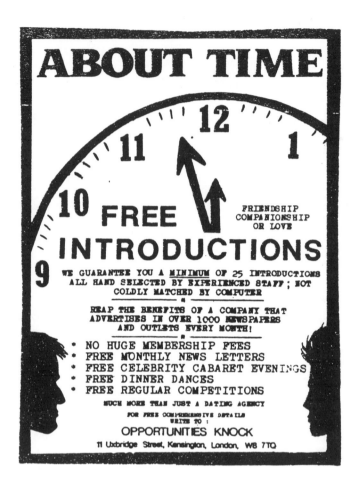

Invite the candidates to comment on

– who the agency might be intended for
– whether the agency is a good idea or not, and why
– whether agencies like this exist in the student's own country
– suggestions for alternative ways lonely people could make friends

Questions such as the following may help to lead the discussion in the right direction.

Who do you think this advertisement is aimed at?
Do you think agencies like this are a good thing? Why?
Can you find agencies like this in your country?
What other ways can you suggest for lonely people to make friends?
What would you do if you moved to a new town and wanted to make friends?

Activity
Refer students to the advertisements for entertainment on page 115 of the Student's Book.

41

ADAM ANT
The Best Childrens entertainment
Fun, Magic, Puppets, Games.
Full catering service available.
Call now for special rates.
01-851 4186.

| ENTERTAINERS | DISCOS |

CHILDRENS ENTERTAINING

Magic * Fun * Songs * Puppets * Games * Prizes.
Entertaining for that special date.
Taking bookings now.
Call 01-207 0930 (24 hours) Danny.

CHILDREN love magic and games by Ron Denton. — Watford (0923) 670610
AUNT POLLY. Childrens entertainer for 4-8 year olds. Fun, magic, games. -Tel. 954-8648.

DYNAMITE DISCOS

For an explosion in sounds.

Book early to avoid disappointment.

Tel. 204-3306

NOW!

A RELIABLE disco available for all occasions many recomendation, reasonable prices, short notice help-out. — Tel. Colin on 368-2921
MOBY DICKS Mobile disco. You tried the rest now try the best. Let your leisure be your pleasure. - Tel. 205-2939 or 205-3011.

THE GOOD OLD DAYS

Songs round the piano!

Jack Boswell will get you
singing the songs ♫
you used to sing. ♫

Tel. 0223 63022

Invite the students to imagine that they have been asked to help organise a social evening for a group of people at their local community centre.
Ask the students to plan the evening for

a) a group of 6–10 year old children
and/or b) a group of 16 year olds
and/or c) a group of old people

Prompts such as the following may prove helpful:

– What kind of entertainment will you choose? Why?
– What time of the day or evening will you hold the 'party'? Why?
– What kind of food and drink do you think will be most suitable? Why?

Optional Reading

Students may choose to base their Interview on one of the three prescribed background texts. Each book stays on the syllabus for two years and may be read as preparation for Paper 5 and/or Paper 2. If a student chooses to talk about one of the books, the format of the interview remains the same as for the general packages, e.g. visual stimulus, passages (for the background texts the passages comprise short extracts from the books) and discussion.

It should be noted that close knowledge of the text and literary appreciation are **not** being tested. The marking criteria and Interview procedure are the same as for the general topics.

L P HARTLEY: *The Go-Between*
The following sample package of oral examiner's material enables a complete Interview to be practised and students' speaking skills to be assessed according to the marking scales given on pages 10–12. The photographs, passages and discussion topics for this package can be found on pages 116–119 of the Student's Book.

Summary

In 1990, when class distinctions were strictly observed, Leo Colston, 12, becomes caught up in the triangle involving the beautiful Marian Maudsley of Brandham Hall, her lover, Ted Burgess, a local farmer and Viscount Trimingham, a Boer War hero whom Marian is expected to marry. The tragic consequences result in Leo's withdrawal from all emotional relationships.

In his sixties, Leo discovers the diary he kept as a schoolboy. It records how he tries to revenge himself on two bullies by casting spells. Coincidentally these two boys have a serious accident. From then on Leo is respected and half believes in his own powers.

Leo is invited by classmate, Marcus Maudsley, to spend a holiday at his home, Brandham Hall in Norfolk. The Maudsleys' opulent lifestyle is totally different from Leo's modest background. It is hot. Marian takes Leo to Norwich to buy him some summer clothes, where she also takes the opportunity to meet Ted. One afternoon, Leo injures his knee sliding down a haystack on Ted's farm. When Ted learns that Leo is a guest at Brandham Hall, he bandages the knee carefully. Leo then agrees to take Marian a secret message and so becomes their 'Go-Between', but it is not until he reads part of an unsealed letter from Marian that he realises they are in love.

At the village cricket match Leo triumphantly catches Ted out and is further acclaimed for his singing at the concert that follows. Afterwards Marcus tells him secretly that Marian is engaged to Viscount Trimingham.

Leo takes a last message from Ted asking Marian to meet him. Believing that Ted has put a spell on Marian, he tells her the wrong time. That night Leo determines to make his own spell from the Belladonna rioting in the outhouse. But he becomes entangled with the plant and escapes with difficulty. The spell to end the affair is never cast.

During Leo's 13th birthday party, Mrs Maudsley becomes suspicious because Marian does not appear. Convinced that Leo knows where she is, she drags him outside to a disused hut in the garden. Here Marian and Ted are discovered making love.

Ted Burgess subsequently shoots himself.

Epilogue
After discovering the diary, the elderly Leo revisits Brandham, where he learns from a now pathetic Marian that the present Viscount is Ted's grandson.

Photographs

Refer student(s) to one or more of the visual prompts on pages 116 and 117 of the Student's Book. Allow assimilation time and then encourage student(s) to respond to the visual material, and relate it to the text-based theme, as in the general package format.

NB As the pictures, passages and discussion topics for text-based packages will inevitably have some similarities, students should be encouraged to speak about different aspects and to add their own feelings and experiences where relevant. Simple repetitions and prepared speeches are insufficient.

42

43

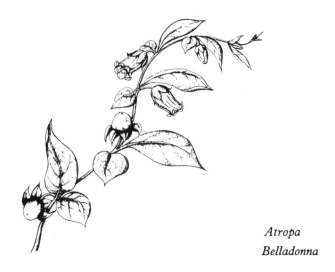

*Atropa
Belladonna*

44

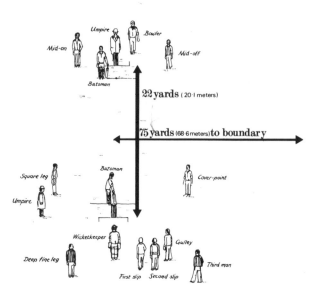

These are the main positions on the cricket field.

The conversation should then lead on to an informal discussion of one or more of the following subjects:

- The story *The Go-Between* has been made into a film. Have you seen the film? If yes, compare and contrast the film and the book. If no, which actors and actresses would you choose to play the main roles and why?
- What is the significance of the cricket match in the book?
- Why is the picture of the belladonna plant included?
- How relevant are the signs of the zodiac to Leo?
- What pictures would you have chosen as visual prompts for this book?

Passages

Ask the students to look at one or more of the passages: Interview Exercises 45–50. Invite comment/reference to content etc. as for the general passages, but within the special scope of the text-based discussion, i.e. identification of character, incident, setting etc., as appropriate. Comments may include an interpretation of or reactions to the text. Follow up any discussion of features of the text which students find typical, unusual or particularly enjoyable.

45 I should have been ashamed of those curses because they were wrong, even wicked perhaps. But I was not ashamed of them then and I am not ashamed of them now. Indeed, I envy the strength of character that I used to have. When I was young, I did not turn away from my enemies. I used to fight them in my own way.

46 I now began to enjoy the hot weather. I liked to feel the heat on my skin. The green suit was made of thin cloth and it had an open neck. My trousers were also open at the knee. My new stockings were hardly thick enough to protect my legs from thorns. But I was especially proud of my new shoes, partly because they were just like Marcus's.

47 I stood up and walked about. My knee was beginning to feel better. I was already planning the story that I should tell Brandham Hall. But I owed something to the farmer. I would not have offered him money even if I had had any. But perhaps I could give him a present. I looked round the bare kitchen. I wondered whether he needed anything.

48 I decided, then, to read it. There were other good arguments in my favour. This letter might be the last that I should deliver. If it was very secret or very important, I would probably carry more in spite of Marcus's presence. If Marian was in danger, she would expect me to read it.

49 I stretched out my hand and touched the flowers and leaves. They held my hand. If I went inside the hut, I should learn its secret. And it would learn mine. I went in. It was hot and soft and comfortable inside. A flower touched my face. Some of the fruit rubbed against my lips . . .

50 Mrs Maudsley said nothing. She ran with wide, awkward steps, and her skirt was dragging through the mud. It was soon clear that she was guiding me. She knew where we were going. When we came to the path between the bushes, I tried to turn her back.

I cried, 'Not this way, Mrs Maudsley!'.

Discussion

For a further exercise choose one or more of the following topics in Interview Exercise 51 for discussion.

51
1 Country house life in 1900

2 Mrs Maudsley

3 Leo's relationship with Ted Burgess

4 The problems of adolescence

5 Lord Trimingham

6 Your general impressions of the book